T0106648

# ALSO BY THE AUTHOR

**From the Flight Deck - Thoughts on Sales, Life and Personal Development (2011)**

# THE SAGE'S JOURNEY

## A Fable about Travelling Your Own Path to Destiny

## ALEX PETTES

 iUniverse®

# THE SAGE'S JOURNEY
# A FABLE ABOUT TRAVELLING YOUR
# OWN PATH TO DESTINY

*Scripture quotations marked NIV are taken from the Holy Bible, New International Version®. NIV®. Copyright © 1973, 1978, 1984 by International Bible Society. Used by permission of Zondervan. All rights reserved. [Biblica]*

*iUniverse books may be ordered through booksellers or by contacting:*

*iUniverse*
*1663 Liberty Drive*
*Bloomington, IN 47403*
*www.iuniverse.com*
*1-800-Authors (1-800-288-4677)*

*ISBN: 978-1-5320-4570-7 (sc)*
*ISBN: 978-1-5320-4571-4 (e)*

*Library of Congress Control Number: 2018905132*

*Print information available on the last page.*

*iUniverse rev. date: 04/25/2018*

# *Dedication*

To my wife Tammy who has enabled me to travel my own Sage's Journey, and with whom I want to spend the rest of the journey with.

# Contents

# *Preface*

Welcome to this adventure of my second book! I self-published my first book, "From the Flight Deck – Thoughts on Sales, Life and Personal Development" in January 2011. I called it a "Best Giver" rather than a "Best Seller" as I never planned to sell any copies. I ended up giving away approximately 1,800 copies and selling about 10. I finished the first book and self-published it when I was forty-four years old. The book was more of a collection of random stories and ideas that were a result of some self-discovery and my need to share some of my ideas I had learned through this "mid-life" review.

Now at fifty-one, it has been a year since I sold my business, and I have spent the past year fully in reflection mode, trying to determine what I will do in this next chapter of my life. Four months prior to selling my business and transitioning the company to the next generation of very capable leadership, I engaged with a coach to work through "what's next." This continued for another nine months after the business was sold and I feel I am in a good spot to work through what will keep me occupied for the next thirty-five or so years. One of the things I wanted to do was to write another book. Thus here we are. I chose a log cabin in the woods beside a lake in a little township called Tiny, which is about an hour north of Barrie, Ontario to start the book. Over an eight-day solo retreat, the book just came out! I have had to spend more time on the editing, but the main book was written during those eight days in January 2018, the wood stove cracking and my fingers flying.

But where to begin? I have been a constant reader and learner, consciously focusing on my own personal and professional development on a non-stop basis for well over twenty-five years. I have read many books, met many people, and have had lots of learning experiences. One of the styles of books I have enjoyed has been where we follow and learn from someone on a journey, and through their journey we take away a few of their lessons as our own. I think of Robin Sharma's "The Monk Who Sold His Ferrari" or Andy Andrews "The Traveler's Gift." Or Spencer Johnson's "Who Moved My Cheese" and Og Mandino's "The Greatest Salesman in the World." So I wrote this book in the style of a fable or story. If nothing else, writing it has been a joy of discovery, reflection and doing my part to share some of the wisdom and ideas I have learned along the way. I hope in some small way this book serves you.

Alex Pettes
March 2018

# *Acknowledgements*

I want to acknowledge a few people who helped me with this project. I want to thank my sister Julia Sadrian for her editing skills and comments that have made this book flow much better than it did without her input. Also, I want to thank my daughter Nicole Pettes who did all the illustrations in the book. She did an excellent job interpreting my comments into some great images! Finally, to Mike Boydell who has worked with me for over seven years, for his insights and support as I travelled my own personal journey.

# The Library

It was in the library where I first met the wise man who would send me on the most fantastic journey I could have ever imagined. His name was Mike. He was sitting by the window in a comfortable chair reading and drinking his green tea. With the internet, why would anyone want to come into a library anymore, to search through a limited inventory of books, during a limited number of hours, let alone leave your house and travel to do it? But Mike like myself found it pleasant to read actual, tangible books, holding the words in one's hand.

I first saw Mike one cold day in January when I was in searching for my next read. He may have been there many times before, but I noticed him that day for the first time. He had a lean athletic build and a youthful countenance that hid his true age. He was sitting in one of the easy chairs by the window. When I sat down on a chair beside him he smiled and said, "Here on the search for wisdom, are you?"

"Something like that," I replied. "I am always on the search for something new, and yes, I would say I am travelling the path to find new ideas."

"That path can be a long one, but it is worthy to be travelled," he replied. "Hi, my name is Mike."

"I'm Dewey, yes Dewey like the Dewey Decimal system," I replied. "When I say that to people under 30, they look at me with this blank stare, as they have no idea what the Dewey Decimal system is, let alone have heard of it."

"The Dewey Decimal System, which became the standard classification system for libraries, was developed by Melvil Dewey in the mid 1870's. He also established the American Metric Bureau in 1876 to try and help promote the metric system throughout America. He also was instrumental in bringing the 1932 Winter Olympics to Lake Placid, New York," Mike responded with a twinkle.

"Impressive!" I said. "I did not know that. Melvil you say was his first name? I am glad my parents didn't name me Melvil!"

"How did you get a name like Dewey in the first place?" Mike asked.

"My grandfather was the chairman of the local library board, and so I guess that is how I came by it. There certainly were never any other kids in school with the same name, so I was unique!" I replied.

"We are all unique, and yet alike in many ways," Mike said. "It is nice to meet you Dewey." Mike noticed I had a book in my hand. "Did you find anything interesting here today?"

"I did find something that might turn out to be interesting," I replied. "I have always been a big reader. I used to start my morning for years with 20-30 minutes of reading. It enabled me to learn lots of things in my field, which was business, and to get many new insights. I got the idea of reading 20 minutes every morning from one of the books I read."

"A book by Brian Tracy, I presume?" he asked. "He called it one of the two best pieces of advice he ever took. Do you know what the other 'best' advice was?"

"Never listen to the radio in your car. Always be listening to audiotapes and turn your car into a university on wheels," I responded. "A fellow Brian Tracy fan! You know, I took both pieces of advice when I was about twenty-five, and have kept it up ever since. That was back in the days of cassette tapes, and I had a big collection. Then tapes became CD's, and now it is on-line podcasts or downloadable books. I still have not progressed to the downloadable stuff; there is something I still like about having something tangible, even if it is a thin silver disc!"

"I am impressed!" said Mike. "I too have been a lifetime student of the science of personal development. Back thousands of years ago the sages of India wrote that the culmination of Supreme Wisdom was very simple, to 'Know Thyself.' Simple to say, but harder to achieve."

I looked at this man sitting beside me in the library. This was certainly not the conversation I was expecting today when I came in. "Intriguing!" I said.

We both smiled and began to read our books. We sat by the window reading for some time until I looked at my watch. Just over an hour had passed.

"Mike, it was a pleasure to meet you," I said. "I have to go, but I hope I see you again."

"I have a feeling we will," said Mike smiling. "Until then…"

I got up and walked to the checkout counter of the library. Little did I know that I would see lots more of Mike, and that he would have such an impact on my life.

# The Sage's Journey

Over the next few months, I continued to see Mike every time I went to the library. I am not sure if he went every day, but I never failed to see him when I was in. We got to know each other quite well, and our conversations deepened each time we met. I never learned more about his background or where he was from. Every time I asked, he just smiled and changed the direction of the conversation. He had this mysteriously elusive quality about him. He asked questions, but never gave answers.

One day he asked me why I was able to spend so much time at the library.

"Well," I replied, "I was able to sell my business about a year ago and reduce my working hours. When I first joined the company, two brothers had run it for over thirty years. The business had grown from one employee to over fifty, and had developed a great reputation, becoming the leader in its industry. My partner and I bought the business about eight years ago, and the business continued to grow until we had almost one hundred employees. Then we saw we had an internal person who had all the right stuff to move the business to the next level. He was ready and able to take over, so we made a deal. I was only fifty when we made this deal, and he has done an excellent job of taking the reins. Now, I am able to spend my time working on the next chapter of my life. That's how I come to be here regularly."

"I am surprised that you were able to walk away from the business at such a young age. Most business owners and executives find it hard to leave the excitement and meaning being in charge brings to their lives. It is often an intoxicating thing to be in control of others, and walking away from this must have been quite difficult," Mike said, looking inquiringly at me.

"I won't say I don't miss it sometimes," I replied. "Being in charge, making decisions, impacting the business and the people I worked with was rewarding. I was conscious, however, never to allow my identity to be so tied up with that role that it became who I am. Don't get me wrong; I loved running the business, but it never became all-consuming. Now I am looking for my next adventure!"

Mike sat there quietly, listening to what I was saying. After a long pause, he said, "It sounds like you are on the Sage's Journey."

"The what? The Sage's Journey?" I laughed. "I may be many things, but I am not a Sage. I am not some wrinkled old guy sitting under a tree giving out pearls of wisdom. Or some Oracle in a cave where people come to find enlightenment."

"I did not say you were a Sage," Mike said. "I said you were on the Sage's Journey."

"The Sage's Journey," he continued, "is the final stage of what is often considered life's journey. Let me try to describe the stages of this journey.

"All people go through a series of stages through their life as they develop and evolve, hoping to learn the lessons that will equip them for the next stage. The first is the Childhood Stage. Here children have adventures, experience new things and discover their world. It is a time where they are affirmed as being loved, prized and important.

"The second stage is the Adventurer Stage. Here you learn that life takes hard work and that it is not soft and comfortable. You make mistakes, overcome problems and learn that through trials, adventures and experiences that you have the confidence to handle what life gives you.

"The next stage is the Warrior Stage. Here you learn that there are things in life worth fighting for, and certain things that must be fought for. You get passionate about a cause and want to make a difference. The heart of the warrior says 'I will not let evil have its way', and they fight for what they believe in. The Warrior, if they are wise, learns the lessons of the battlefield: fight one battle at a time, and fight the battle once. Don't continually fight the same battle over and over, worrying that you are never done. If you are tempted, resist it quickly and stay with the battle. Remain strong and keep persisting in fighting for what you believe; never give up!

"The fourth stage on the journey is the Lover. It is here that the soul awakens to beauty, in people and in nature, and it stirs them to serve others. You grow and serve your family, your passions and try to apply all the lessons from the other stages as you now start to help others as they begin their own journeys.

"The next stage and aim of the journey is to have equipped the person to become the Leader. What is the Leader? A Leader has power over others, and hopefully the journey has prepared them to handle this power. Many times this power consumes and the Leader does not do good, but evil. True Leaders are reluctant to seize this power, but do it on behalf of others, so they may serve them. The true test of a Leader is what life is like for those under his or her authority. Do the people prosper and grow, or suffer. The Leader does not have to control many people, it may be just a small group. And when I say 'lead', I don't mean dominate or control. A wise Leader knows that their job is to make those he or she influences grow, develop and prosper as their own persons, not in the image or way the Leader thinks they should be. Being a Leader is a great responsibility.

"The sixth and final stage, and the path that few find themselves on, is the Sage's Journey. It is here that the Leader has relinquished or given up his control, and instead searches for wisdom and insight so that he may provide this to others. We often think of Sages as the wise elders of the community, but old age does not automatically make you a Sage. It is the attitude and wisdom to focus on others and their service that defines a true Sage."

With that long explanation finished, Mike looked at me, waiting for a reaction. I replied, "Well, you certainly seem to have life all figured out! I am not sure life is a simple series of stages that you go through, and I am not sure I am ready to become a Sage! I am too young and really not that wise! And besides, how do you travel this Sage's Journey?"

Mike replied, "Not everyone progresses through the stages. Often they remain trapped in one stage for their entire lives. They don't learn the lessons and move forward for a variety of reasons. But I am not interested in everyone; I am interested in you. And if you allow me to be a guide for you, I think you may well progress along the journey to eventually becoming a Sage."

I looked at him for a long time. Who was this guy from the library to offer to be my 'tour guide'? "I will think about it Mike, thanks."

With that, I collected my things and got up to leave. "I will see you soon," said Mike. "Think about what I said. I hope you will consider this journey to be worthy of you and your effort." And with that, he smiled at me and went back to his book.

# The Magic Coin

A month or so had gone by since Mike had talked to me about the Sage's Journey. I had been to the library since then and had sat with Mike each time, but neither he nor I brought it up. I often reflected upon what he had said during that time. What was I looking for? What journey was I on? Life was pretty good and I was enjoying this time of 'retirement'. But something kept pulling me back to this idea of the Sage's Journey. I had always been looking for something to make myself better. Mike's first words to me at the library were "Here on the search for wisdom, are you?" Perhaps I was already on this journey, I just did not know it.

So the next time I saw Mike, I sat down and said, "So tell me, what is involved in this Sage's Journey? And why do you want to be my tour guide?"

Mike put his book down and looked thoughtfully at me. "Well, you seem ready to talk about the Sage's Journey. I was wondering if you were going to bring it up."

"I have thought about what you said, and something resonated with me," I responded. "I think I have always been on the search for something deeper and more meaningful. I think my job as President allowed me to play the role of the Leader. I was responsible for others, tried to do what I could to grow the people and the business, and I feel that I left the company better off than when I found it. Now that I am no longer involved day to day, I wonder what is next. And you say it is the Sage's Journey. I am not sure I am a Sage, or will ever be one, but maybe this journey you talk about could be the next step for me."

Mike smiled. "'A journey of a thousand leagues begins with a single step'. If you allow me, I think I can help you; be your 'tour guide' so to speak. However, this journey you will do alone. I can do my best to aid you on your journey, but the Sage's Journey is unique and different for all who travel it." Mike paused for a moment before continuing. "I will help you. I need to prepare for this, so let's agree to meet back here tomorrow at this same time. If that is agreeable to you, I will leave now and prepare. Are you willing to allow me to aid you?"

"I will see you tomorrow, same time, same place!" I said to Mike. Mike got up, smiled and walked out of the library.

The next day as I was walking up to the library, I saw Mike waiting on the steps for me. "Let's go for a walk and find a private place to talk," he said. "Not that the library is not a quiet place, but let's find a bench outside where we can talk undisturbed." So we started walking until we found a bench in a local park. There were no other benches near us, and the park was quiet. As we went to sit down, I noticed a small, stainless steel plaque in the middle of the top slat on the back of the bench. It read "DONATED IN LOVING MEMORY OF VILMA STEPHANIE HEFLER (BOBBY) 1921 – 2003 WHO LOVED THIS PARK."

DONATED IN LOVING MEMORY OF
VILMA STEPHANIE HEFLER (BOBBY) 1921-2003
WHO LOVED THIS PARK

"I wonder who this 'Bobby' person was?" I asked out loud. "I don't know," said Mike, "but I don't think Bobby will mind if we sit on her bench." We sat down and Mike began to speak.

"Throughout our life, we have met many different people. Some are friends or classmates. Others are family members, teachers, co-workers or bosses. Others are just characters or authors we met only in books or movies. Some have had strong and lasting impacts on us; others not so much. But most of what we have learned and become is the result of these interactions. We are all born with a unique genetic disposition, but I like to think that the choices we make, as well as the people we meet and learn from have a stronger influence of who we are at this moment.

"The journey you are about to take will involve you meeting and talking to different people. 'Wisdom and learning are not given, they are taken', a wise Swami once said. The people you will get to meet will each leave you with something. Sometimes it will be an item, a symbol from which to remind you of what you have learned. Other times it may well be a simple feeling or word that you take. As you travel this journey, allow yourself to be open to listen, and to reflect on what you see and hear. This journey is yours alone to travel. And this Sage's Journey is unique in that it will not come to an end. As you start on this journey, you will never come to the end of the road and know that it is finished. It is the joy of the journey that never ends that is the reward. It is enough to find joy in travelling the journey, not in reaching a final destination. That same Swami said, 'To strive, to struggle, not to succeed – make this your motto in life.'"

With that, Mike reached into his pocket and pulled out a coin. It was about 2" in diameter, blue and red and had a bunch of markings and words on it. "Is that some special challenge coin?" I asked. I knew the military tradition of carrying a coin with your unit's insignia on it had started in World War One when a wealthy officer in a flying squadron had coins minted with the squadron's insignia on it. "Not exactly," he said. "It is called an Axiom coin."

"What is the difference?" I asked, intrigued. I had never heard of an Axiom coin.

"An Axiom is defined as a self-evident truth that requires no proof. It is a principle or statement that everyone believes is true. This one is a special Destiny coin. Here, take a look," he said as he handed me the coin.

I took the coin in my hand and examined it. The main feature was a red and blue navigator star, with a key on each of the West and East points of the star. The North point had the word 'Destiny', and all around the outside edge were a number of stars. Inscribed inside the ring created by the stars were the words 'Within Realm of All Possibilities.'

I turned the coin over. On the outside edge in Roman numerals were the numbers 1-12, all in the positions you would expect on a clock face. Inside the ring created by the numbers was a quote. 'Destiny is not a matter of chance, it is a matter of choice; it is not a thing to be waited for, it is a thing to be achieved.'

"Very nice," I said handing the coin back to him.

"No, keep it, it's yours," replied Mike. "This is a very special coin, with lots of meaning and significance. Let me explain.

"The Navigational Star serves as a reminder to listen to our internal guidance system, or conscience, in all we do. The keys at West and East represent the ability to unlock both your mind and your potential. The words on this face remind us that your destiny is within the realm of all possibilities! The stars that encompass the edge symbolize our infinite possibilities as well as the endless universe we have within which we may grow.

"On the other side, the clock face without hands is to remind us that we live only in the now, not the future. The quote is from Williams Jennings Bryan, who was the US Secretary of State from 1913-1915. It says that your destiny is not a simple matter of chance, but something that action and your choices determine."

"Wow, that's pretty deep stuff for a simple coin!" I exclaimed. "Thank you for giving it to me."

"This coin is more than just a simple token," Mike said. "It is small enough to carry in your pocket, always there to remind you that you are responsible for your actions and that your choices of what you do or don't do will shape your eventual destiny. It will serve you well on your journey. Plus," he said with a twinkle, "this coin is magic!"

"A magic coin!" I laughed at the idea. But the look on Mike's face told me he was serious about what he had said. "OK, how does this magic coin work? What does it do?"

Mike looked at me with a thoughtful expression. "Very few people are given the chance that you are about to be given. This magic coin will serve to allow you to meet with and talk to many people who have walked this journey before you. I hope that as you meet them, you choose to accept whatever they may offer you. As you travel this Sage's Journey, collecting insight and wisdom, I hope what you learn you will share with others, thus helping them travel their own journey. The ability to help others progress on their own path is the role of the Sage. There are different types of Sages, and each is unique in what lessons they may offer. You must discover what path and what gifts you have that will help others. This coin will serve to introduce you to the people you will meet along your path, and show them you are one of the special few who have been given this privilege."

I took all of this in. A magic coin with special powers!? It all seemed to be too fantastic to believe. Yet something about Mike made me believe what he was saying. To this day, I still don't know why I believed him, but the journey was about to begin with that simple coin.

# Rumi – What Path to Walk?

"I know this idea of a magic coin is a lot to take in," said Mike. "I will give you a few days to think about what I have said, and if you are interested in learning more, let's meet at the same time next week, here at this same spot in the park." I agreed and we parted. I was not sure what I believed, but a week later I was back at 'Bobby's' bench in the park.

"I am pleased you are ready to continue on your journey of self-discovery," said Mike. "My role as your 'tour guide' will be to introduce you to certain people. You will be on your own when you meet them, and each has something unique to offer. Are you ready to begin?"

"So how will all this work," I asked. "How do I meet these people, and what do I do with this so-called magic coin?"

"It is easier than you may think," Mike said. "Each time we get together, I will prepare you before your meeting with each of them. We will meet here at the same time each week. After our discussion, you will go to bed that night with the coin in your hand. The coin will allow you to make contact with each person. When you awaken the next morning, you are to write down what comes to your mind. Take this learning with you as you continue on your journey. It is all in your hands. My role is simply to make introductions. This is your individual journey, and I do not want to influence your path. Do you understand?"

"I think so. Since I have been sixteen, I have been keeping a journal. I have always felt that a life worth living is a life worth recording." I was intrigued and ready to get started.

"Alright, let's begin," said Mike. "Have you ever heard of Rumi?"

"Hmm, maybe. Wasn't he a poet?" I replied.

"He was, and so much more," continued Mike. "He was a 13th-century Persian poet and spiritual thinker. He grew up in what is now Afghanistan and was a wise, thoughtful and insightful thinker. He believed that people of all religions and backgrounds could live together in peace and harmony. His poetry spoke of the higher callings we all yearn for, that of inner peace and happiness.

"He wrote a simple poem that echo's the verse on your coin, that destiny is a matter of choice.

'If you want money more than anything,
you will be bought and sold.

If you have a greed for food,
you will become a loaf of bread.

This is a subtle truth.
Whatever you love, you are.'

"His influence has transcended time, as well as many national and ethnic borders. Iranians, Turks, Greeks and many South and Central Asian Muslims have all appreciated his spiritual legacy for over seven centuries. He is a worthy first visitor for you."

"Well, I don't know what I will learn from someone dead over 700 years, but I will trust your judgment," I replied. "So I just fall asleep with the coin in my hand tonight, that's it?"

"That's it," said Mike. "When you awake, make notes in your journal. Think of what he has said, and reflect upon this. When we meet again next week, I will introduce you to someone else." With that, Mike got up from the bench, smiled at me and walked away.

For the rest of the day, I did not know what to expect. I was curious but did not really believe that somehow I would be transported back in time to meet a long-dead Middle Eastern mystic! That night, as I went to bed, I put the

Destiny coin in my hand. I looked at the gold lettering on this blue and red coin and soon fell asleep.

I awoke in what appeared to be a small vegetable stall in a large market. I stood up, bewildered as to why I would be in a vegetable stall. There were many men and women in the market. My nose was filled with the earthy smells of vegetables, sweets and animals. I looked around but did not recognize where I was.

I began to walk through the market amidst the noise and jostling of people arguing with the shopkeepers and stall owners. I came upon a man sitting near a pool of water. Beside him was a large stack of scrolls. He was engrossed in his reading, but somehow I knew it was him!

"What are you reading?" I asked him.

"Something you cannot understand," the man scoffingly replied. He returned to his reading.

I continued to stare at him. He looked up at me. "What is it that you want?" he asked in a gruff voice.

"I am looking for he who is called Rumi. Are you him?" I asked.

"Who is it that looks for Rumi?" he asked? Not knowing how to say I was a visitor from the future, I remembered the coin in my hand. I handed him the coin.

As he took the coin in his hand, his eyes widened and he looked me in the eyes. "It is I, Rumi, that you seek. How may I serve you?" he asked as he returned the coin to me.

"I was hoping you could help me. I am travelling what I have been told is the Sage's Journey, and was sent to speak with you," I replied. "What I am to ask you or what you are to tell me, I don't know."

"Let us go inside and talk," Rumi replied, rising from his reading and motioning me to follow him into a small house. Once inside, he showed me to a table with four chairs. He indicated that I should sit, and he went and got a jug of water with two goblets. As he poured the water, I sat down and waited for him to finish. The jug and the goblets were made of plain glazed clay, and had no ornamentation or markings.

He sat down and picked up his goblet of water. After saying a few words I could not understand, he drank from his goblet and put it down. Looking at me he said, "So you are travelling the Sage's Journey. This is good. I see you are one of those who travels with the coin of Destiny." He smiled. "Have you determined the primary path of your journey?"

"The primary path? Is there a special path I am supposed to be travelling on? I don't know what the primary path is or even what path I am on!" I said.

"As we travel along the path to helping others; which is the true meaning of the Sage's Journey; there are three primary paths. Most can travel only one path, others can travel two paths at the same time. No one should travel all three paths, as this lack of focus will not prove fruitful for either the one on the path, or the ones he wishes to serve," Rumi replied.

"How do I know where to find these paths, or which path I am on?" I asked.

Rumi replied, "Be a lamp, a ladder, a lifeboat."

"I do not understand," I said. "What are these paths you are talking about?"

"Be a lamp, a ladder, a lifeboat," he replied once again. With that simple phrase, he rose and walked toward the door. "I wish you well on your journey. I am blessed to have had you share my home and my table. Goodbye."

With that, he walked out of the door. I tried to follow him, but when I got to the door and walked through, I found myself awake in my room.

# A Lamp, A Ladder,
# A Lifeboat

As I awoke from my visit with Rumi, I remembered what Mike said about recording what I learned in my journal. I grabbed my journal and wrote the only advice that Rumi had given me. 'Be a Lamp, a Ladder, a Lifeboat.' That was it. He had asked what path I was on, so I wrote down 'What path to travel?' It was such a brief visit, and I wondered what to make of these three items he had talked about.

I thought about his comment that there are three paths, and you should only travel one, maybe two, but not all of them. Then the only thing he told me was 'Be a Lamp, a Ladder, a Lifeboat.' Maybe these items represented the various paths of the Sage's Journey. As I reflected on these,

I thought about what each item (each maybe representing a path?) might mean to me.

"A Lamp," I said out loud to myself. I began trying to figure this out. What is a lamp? Back in Rumi's time there were no electric lamps, just oil lamps. So what and how does an oil lamp work? Well, it has a housing, a wick, it needs fuel to work, and then a source of ignition to light it. The lamp will give off light and maybe some heat. But a lamp will only light up a room or part of a room. If you run out of fuel, the lamp does not work. And occasionally you have to trim the wick to make it more efficient. But what kind of path is a lamp?

I shook my head and started to think about the next thing Rumi had said. "What does a ladder have to do with a path?" I wondered out loud to myself. I had a habit of talking out loud to myself; it helped me to think. "Well, a ladder can be made of a different types of materials; wood, metal, plastic; no, not plastic, Rumi would not have had plastic. It has rungs spaced out for you to step on. Ladders are designed to help you climb up to a spot higher that you can reach. Ladders are usually sturdy and reliable, but you don't spend much time on a ladder. Once you climb up and get what you want, you get off them and put them away. Ladders are often a metaphor for advancing your career, 'climbing the corporate ladder.'"

I laughed as I remembered a joke I had heard about climbing the corporate ladder. I could not remember who said it, but I remember it was in one of the leadership books I had read. 'The chain of command in any organization is like a tree full of monkeys. If you look down from the top, all you see are smiling faces. If you look up from the bottom, you get a much different perspective!'

I then thought about Rumi's comment about being a lifeboat. What is a lifeboat? Well, it is usually a small rescue craft that bobs through the seas toward the people who have either fallen off the ship and are swimming in the water, or it is going to rescue those still on the sinking ship. It is smaller than the ship and can hold a few people. A lifeboat heading toward those in need is perceived with joy and relief by those who see it coming toward them. The lifeboat must have someone rowing toward them, and then the rescuers must lean over into the water to grab those in need and pull them aboard to safety. But without this lifeboat to help them, the people who need them would most likely perish. But not everyone who needs the lifeboat may be able to either climb aboard or be able to get to in if the lifeboat is already full. "Hmm," I said to myself, "interesting..." After some reflection, I started to make notes in my journal.

> Lamp: I like the idea of being a lamp. Someone who can help show the way, dispel the darkness to those near me. I remembered a quote I had read; "He who receives an idea from me receives instruction himself without lessening mine; as he who lights his taper at mine receives light without darkening me." With a lamp, although you can only see a few feet in front of you, you can walk 1,000 miles like that. To be a lamp, you need to make sure you don't run out of fuel,

occasionally trim your wick to keep being useful (and not just smoky) and protect the flame from being blown out.

Ladder: A ladder, yes. I enjoy helping others climb into new learning experiences and moving up. Can I see me holding, building or providing these ladders? What or where is 'up?' Time spent on the ladder is short, but crucial to upward movement, especially if you come upon a wall or barrier that you need to scale. Do I carry you up the ladder or just make it available, or show you how to make your own ladder? Interesting thoughts to consider.

Lifeboat: Hmm, probably not. I don't think I am inclined towards 'saving' others. My bent has always been to help others go from good to better; from better to excellent. Many philanthropic causes are worthy ways to help people. I believe in supporting those causes, but I don't know if that is my role to be the lifeboat...

I closed my journal and put it away, allowing the thoughts I had written to simmer in my mind. I did not open the journal for the next few days, allowing myself time to think about what I had learned. Finally, I opened up the journal and made the following entry:

As I think of these three concepts; lamp, ladder, lifeboat; and consider which might be the 'path' I was meant to take, I think that the one that resonates with me the most is the idea of the lamp. I am not a 'lifeboat person', I realize that. I learned long ago to focus on making my strengths stronger rather than trying to build upon a weakness, thereby being 'mediocre' at everything. Strength builds on strength.

I like the idea of the lamp path. Continually refresh and recharge the 'oil' or fuel for the lamp; find new ways to make myself better (trim my wick for optimum performance); provide light, guidance, and ideas to help others. If they learn from me (light their own taper at mine), then more light shines and the path for all get brighter. This fits with who I am; I can see me doing this. I also think it is a long-term idea that could last my whole life.

I also like the idea of the ladder, being able to help people make a 'leap' or climb up to the next level, whatever that level may be. I am not the genius who knows what is on the next level, or even if it is the best idea to climb up to that level, but if I can help, for even a short time...

Lamp, Ladder... that feels right...

With that, I closed my journal and put it back on the shelf. I felt good about where I was, and I wondered whom Mike was going to have me meet next?

# The Trident

I was sitting on the same 'Bobby' bench in the park when Mike came up a few days later. "You must have had a good experience to be keen enough to be waiting for me!" Mike laughed as he shook my hand and sat down. "How was your visit?" he asked.

"Well, I have to tell you honestly that I was not sure about this whole 'magic coin' and time travel thing," I replied. "But somehow it worked, and I had a brief but meaningful interaction with Rumi. He spoke about choosing the primary path for my journey. I know you don't want to discuss what I learned, so all I am going to say is 'Lamp, Ladder.'"

"Interesting!" Mike said. "It sounds like you have some clarity and direction for yourself. Selection is all about de-selection, and what we do is almost as important as what we choose not to do. I am glad you have made some choices."

"I have, and I feel good about them," I said. "Now, who do you have in mind next? Am I going to travel back in time again?"

"No, not this time," said Mike. "This next person happens to be in town for the next few days, and I have arranged for you to meet him. His name is Rob Roy, and he is a retired Leading Chief Petty Officer of the US Navy SEALs."

"Wow! A Navy SEAL! What does he have to do with walking the Sage's Journey?" I asked.

"Let me tell you a little about Rob, and when you meet him, maybe he will answer that question," Mike said.

"Rob is a twenty-six year veteran of the US Navy, spending twenty years as a Navy SEAL. He was involved with some of the most active units in the SEALs. He led teams in harm's way and served in some of the most hostile parts of the world. After he retired, he started his own consulting company, and has been a long time military consultant for the Play Station 'SOCOM – US Navy Seals' video game franchise since 2002, appearing on both of the covers of the SOCOM and SOCOM II video game jackets! He now has a company that uses the lessons and experiences he got in the SEAL teams to help individuals and companies become better leaders and teams. He is here working with a client, but I have arranged for you to meet with him tomorrow."

"OK, I am excited to meet him," I said. "Just let me know where and when."

Mike handed me a piece of paper with the details about my meeting with Rob. I thanked him and got up to leave. "I appreciate this Mike," I said. "I will meet him, and we will meet again next week, right? Same time, same place?"

"Same time, same place," said Mike. "I hope you enjoy your time with him."

I met Rob the next day in the lobby of a downtown hotel where he was preparing to give a seminar later that afternoon. We sat down in the coffee shop of the hotel and began to talk.

"Hi, I'm Dewey," I said. "Thanks for meeting me here. Did Mike tell you why you should meet with me?"

"He didn't tell me much," Rob replied. "Mike and I are old friends. He attended one of the first events I did back in 2008. We called it 'Leadership Under Fire', and we put all these executives and leaders through a weekend of tough training and exercises, all designed to see how they worked as a team. They got to play in the ocean surf, roll around in the sand, and with their small teams we call 'boat crews', they ran in the sand with logs and even got to paddle a small inflatable boat in the surf. Good fun!" He smiled as he finished.

"That does not sound like fun at all! It sounds like a tough weekend!" I said.

"It was tough, but so is life. Leadership of teams is tough, and these guys all lead teams of various sizes so they knew what they were getting into. Facing challenges as a team, working together, finding the strengths of each of the members and using those strengths to your best advantage; all great lessons for business and life," Rob said thoughtfully. "But the biggest and toughest leadership challenge of all is self-leadership. Doing what you know you should do, persevering through adversity and dealing with all that life throws at you. Taking charge of your life and the choices it gives you. Having a good attitude and outlook is also important."

I reached into my pocket and showed him the back of my Destiny coin with the text about Destiny being a matter of choice. "The choices we make really do shape who we become and how we live our lives," I said. "Mike gave me this coin to remind me of that as I travel my own journey."

Rob studied the coin carefully, turning it over and looking at all the symbols and words. He handed it back to me.

"That is a good coin," he said. "I like all the elements, each one with its own meaning, working together. I also carry a coin with me." He reached into his pocket and pulled out a gold oblong coin.

"As you can see," Rob continued, "on this side is an image of a SEAL operator with his rifle and underwater breathing gear on underneath the SEAL motto, 'The Only Easy Day was Yesterday'. And when you turn it over, there is the Trident insignia of the Navy SEALs. It is an eagle clutching in its talons the trident, a flintlock pistol and a Navy Anchor. Each symbol means something to a SEAL.

"The anchor symbolizes the Navy, and it is an old style anchor, reminding us that our roots lie in the accomplishments of those teams that came before us. The trident symbolizes the SEALs connection to the sea. The ocean is one of the hardest elements for any warrior to operate in, and a SEAL is to be most comfortable with the hardest task. The pistol represents a SEALs capability on land. It is cocked and ready, a reminder that we must be ready at all times. The eagle symbolizes our ability to insert from the air swiftly. Notice that the eagle's head is lowered, not upright like in most all other depictions of this noble bird. It reminds us that humility is the true measure of a warrior's strength."

He offered me the coin to examine. "Wow," I said. "This simple image sure has a lot of meaning. Thank you for explaining it to me." I handed him back the coin.

"Most people when they think of the SEALs have an image of a SEAL as the ultimate warrior; professional, effective, deadly. But SEALs spend much more time training and preparing to fight than actually fighting. To me there are three key things that SEALs know and practice every day that can apply to anyone who wants to prepare for whatever battles life may put in front of them," Rob said, pausing. "These three key things are a solid and clear mind; a fit and capable body, and above all a strong, positive attitude. Mind – Body – Attitude; these three together will help you defeat any enemy, and help you avoid the setbacks and pitfalls that derail weaker individuals."

"Mind – Body – Attitude; those are powerful yet simple ideas," I said to Rob. "These seem to be foundational, simple ideas that anyone can use, not just SEALs!"

"You're right!" Rob said. "A strong mind gives you the ability to quickly observe what is happening, orient your thinking, decide what to do and then act! A strong body is the foundation for keeping your mind sharp. Plus your body is the tool that allows you to direct your actions and move! Having a fit and capable body is something we take for granted until we don't have it. That's why SEALs spend so much time training and working out, so we have the energy and stamina to do what we need. Vince Lombardi famously said 'Fatigue makes cowards of us all.' Taking care of your body so it can take care of you is key.

"And finally, a strong, positive attitude allows you to look past any setbacks and keep moving forward. I don't know who said this but a good attitude is like mining for gold. You have to move tons of dirt to find a single ounce of gold, but you don't go in looking for the dirt, you go in looking for the gold! We often have no control over what happens to us in life. But what we can control is how we REACT to what happens to us in life. A strong, positive attitude can help us deal with and work through any tough circumstances we may come across."

"Well Dewey," Rob said getting up from his chair, "it was a pleasure to meet you. I have to get back and get ready for my group this afternoon. Good luck to you!"

With that he shook my hand and left the coffee shop.

I sat down and reflected on what he had said. I was glad that I had decided to bring my journal with me as I reached into my bag to get it. I opened it up and began to write.

> Rob Roy, Navy SEAL.
>
> The SEAL trident has more meaning than I thought. I like his idea of the three key items that work not only for SEALs but for everyone; a solid and clear Mind; a fit and capable Body; and a positive mental Attitude. Mind, Body, Attitude; MBA! No, MBA sounds too business like, and this is not about business.
>
> But I like the fact that there are three prongs on a trident, and these 3 ideas could represent each of the prongs. But the trident also has a long shaft that directs

and holds the prongs. What are the keys underlying the ideas Rob shared?

Well, it's common knowledge to take care of your body. Nothing earth-shattering here! Diet, exercise, get in shape, keep healthy, eat right, gets lots of sleep; nothing new in that. His idea that the toughest leadership of all is self-leadership is an interesting thought. We all know we should take care of our body, eat right, etc., so why don't we? We just don't have the discipline!

I thought more about what I had just written. Then I had a flash of insight. I drew a picture of a Trident in my journal, the three-pronged spear, with barbs on the end of each prong. I labeled each of the prongs as Mind, Body and Attitude. And I labeled the shaft of the spear as Discipline. I sat back, thinking of this. Not bad Dewey! It was making sense.

I put my journal away and headed home. I felt good about my meeting with Rob and having this trident as a symbol of what I had learned. It was good, but not good enough. What was I missing? I decided to let it simmer for a few days and maybe something would come to my mind.

Two days later as I was thinking of this trident symbol, I had some thoughts. I decided to pull out my journal. I sat there thinking for about 10 minutes, pen in hand. Then I started to write.

I like the symbol of the trident. Simple, elegant and the trident is a strong, unusual weapon. But to label the three prongs as Mind, Body and Attitude just seems incomplete. I like the strong shaft of the trident being represented by Discipline, that underlying strength of character to do what you need to do when you need to do it. How do you have a strong Mind and Body? Good health is key, and the fitness of a SEAL is unquestionable. Hmm...

Then from where I don't know, an idea came to me.

Label each of the three prongs of the trident as Health, Energy, and Fitness. Have the two outside prongs be labeled Health and Fitness. Health is having a body without disease or discomfort. Fitness is your ability to do work and effort. A healthy and fit body gives you energy, the mental and physical fuel to do the work you need to do. All connected together and strengthened by the strong shaft of Discipline. Discipline to eat and stay Healthy. Discipline to keep your body Fit. Discipline to think positive. The shaft of Discipline directly connected to the middle prong of energy, as Health and Fitness join at the base of the middle prong to create Energy! I like it, I like it a lot!

Under this text I drew a trident. Health, Energy, and Fitness were the three prongs, and the shaft represented Discipline. As I was to walk along the Sage's Journey, I would need the discipline to continue on this path. Taking care of myself by keeping my body healthy and fit would translate into the energy I needed to succeed and achieve whatever destiny lay ahead. This also seemed to tie into the idea of my lamp needing to be kept full of fuel. A strong mind, a fit body and a good attitude all would contribute to the energy I would need as I traveled this journey.

I sat back and considered what I had written and this now newly labeled trident. It just seemed right. "Thank you Rob for your inspiration," I said out loud to myself. I closed the journal, put it away, and smiled.

# The Ring

When I arrived in the park the following week to meet Mike, I found him already sitting there on 'Bobby's' bench, waiting for me. He rose and shook my hand as I came up to him and we both sat down.

"What did you think of Rob?" he asked? "Did you enjoy your visit with him?"

"I sure did," I said. "He gave me some great ideas on what it took to succeed not only as a Navy SEAL, but also as a person on whatever path you may be on. It's all about having the discipline to take care of your body, your mind, and guard your attitude. This gives you energy! Simple yet powerful ideas."

"Well I am glad you enjoyed meeting him," Mike said. "I must say when I first met him in 2008, I would not have described what he put us through as 'pleasant', but I am very glad I was able to spend time with him myself."

"I have been thinking about your next visit," Mike continued. "I know that Rumi has helped you identify how you may best serve others along your journey. I hope that your time with Rob helped you realize that service to yourself, physically, mentally, and emotionally help to ensure you don't stumble along your journey.

"Your next visitor is someone you probably have never heard of. His name is Pierre le Tessier du Montarsy."

"Got that right," I said. "Never heard of him. He sounds French."

"He is indeed French, and was one of the most trusted and respected designers to the court of the French King Louis XIV," responded Mike.

"A French designer, interesting! Louis XIV was famous for his extravagance, his clothing and the architecture and furnishings from his palace. Was this Pierre person an architect?" I asked.

"No, he worked with gold and precious gems. He was a jewelry designer," said Mike. "He was known for making Louis the Sun King's glittering fantasies come true. He was a master craftsman with a gift for turning ideas into beautiful works of art. What is not as well known is that Pierre was also a member of the 'Compagnons du Tour de

France'. These Compagnons were artisans and craftsmen who were required as part of their technical education to work as apprentices to masters throughout France, thus taking the 'Tour de France' as they travelled on their journey to becoming masters. And no, it has nothing to do with the cycling Tour de France! Once the apprentices had become masters, they could choose where they wanted to live and were able to then begin to teach what they had learned to a new generation of apprentices. To become a master themselves, after their five years or so of travelling and learning their craft, these apprentices were required to present a 'masterpiece' of their work, thus proving they were worthy to become a full master Compagnon."

"Sounds like an interesting visit," I said. "So do I just do the same thing as when I met Rumi, fall asleep with the coin in my hand?"

"Yes, but there is more that is required of you for this visit," replied Mike. "Pierre will be expecting you to present your own 'masterpiece', or at least your idea for a masterpiece to him. He is one of the most senior and well-respected members of the Compagnons, so speaking to a mere junior apprentice is not something he normally does. He is one of the council who recommends potential new masters. You will need to have thoughtfully considered what your masterpiece will be. It should be something that you have learned or wish to help you as you continue your Sage's Journey. Take a few days to consider what you want to present to him, then fall asleep with the coin. I wish you 'Bon Chance' as you prepare for this next visit!"

With that, Mike got up, shook my hand warmly, and walked away. I was left sitting on the bench, thinking to myself, 'What masterpiece can I present? I am not a jewelry designer; I don't even wear jewelry!' I got up and left, thinking about what you present to a man who creates beauty for a king!

Over the next few days, I thought more about what Mike had said, and what I was going to present as a masterpiece to the Master Jeweler of Louis the XIV! I started to look back at my old journals to try and find some inspiration for what I might want to present. After spending about four hours reading old notes and thoughts, I picked up my journal and started to write. I knew I worked best when I wrote out my thoughts and let them grow.

> What do I present as a masterpiece? Pierre is a master jeweler, so what kind of jewelry should I present? A necklace, bracelet, brooch, earrings... If this is for me, what is a masculine piece of jewelry... a ring! Men's rings are always strong and powerful, and rings have been a symbol of strength and authority for millennia. In the middle ages, rings were often used to seal important documents, as the ring was set into melted wax and the rings impression was then embedded as the wax hardened. Yes, a signet ring! That reminds me of the famous Theodore Tilton poem, 'Even This Shall Pass Away'.

Once in Persia reigned a king;
Who upon his signet ring;
Graved a maxim true and wise;
Which if held before his eyes;
Gave him counsel, at a glance;
Fit for any change or chance;
Solemn words and these are they;
Even This Shall Pass Away.

Yes, a signet ring. So what should the ring be made of? Silver, gold, platinum? Jewels or a diamond? Probably gold; it's a classic and won't tarnish. A diamond?

What should be on the face of this signet ring? Probably a coat of arms, or a seal of some sort. But I don't have a coat of arms, and I think I want to present something that has meaning to me, not just a random lion or gryphon or stag, or other random symbol. Hmm...

I put my pen down. What symbol had meaning to me? Then I remembered the story of the hummingbird.

The forest where the hummingbird lived was on fire! All of the animals ran from the forest and sat watching their home burn. But the hummingbird kept flying from a small stream into the fire with a drop of water in its beak. Back and forth from the stream into the fire it went. The animals began to laugh at the hummingbird.

"What difference are you making?" they all said. The hummingbird replied, "I'm doing all I can."

That story always resonated with me; to do all you can. Not being able to solve or fix a problem is no excuse for not doing all you can. A hummingbird was often seen in First Nations art as a symbol of positivity and as a guide through life's challenges. The hummingbird! I picked up my pen and began to write again.

I think it is a hummingbird. Do all you can, live positively, be full of energy. I like it!
Do I have the hummingbird at a flower with a ruby or other gem to accent it? I will have to think about this.

What else is important to me? My family. I remember when the girls got matching tattoos. An infinity symbol with an anchor embedded in it, and under the infinity symbol was the word 'Promise', to signify that they would always be strong for each other. This is a powerful symbol, and perhaps the anchor ties into the strength and remembering those who came before us, as in the Navy Seal anchor. Yes, I like it. There is something else, I think. What is the final finishing touch? I will have to reflect on this.

As I read what I had just written, I was pleased with this start. Writing in my journal in this style of talking out loud to myself has always helped me think and clarify my ideas. 'Let it simmer, and come back to it tomorrow Dewey,' I said to myself, as put my pen down and closed the journal.

The next morning, I made myself a coffee and sat down with my journal. I had been thinking about the ring overnight, and I thought I had an idea that might work. So I began to write again.

> A trident! I think somehow I should incorporate a trident. I already wrote about the strong meaning of the trident, and the foundational ideas of having the discipline to take care of myself so I can travel the journey and have the strength to be of service to others. A trident is simple and yet powerful. Now to try and incorporate all these elements into something a master jeweler would accept...

I closed the journal. "Tonight we meet, Pierre!" I said out loud to myself. "Let's hope I am ready!"

I fell asleep that night, coin in my hand and ready for this next visit. As I awoke, I found myself sitting in a chair in a formal, ornamental room. My chair was high-backed with gilded legs, and the upholstery was a beautiful crimson silk. Amazed, I looked around this room, with its polished oak shelves heavy with books; a massive, ornately carved gilded cabinet inlaid with what looked like ebony; and a large crackled mirror, the frame resplendent with reclining cherubs. As I turned to look around, I noticed that the top of my chair had the image of a man's face carved into the dark wood, surrounded by what seemed like an oak laurel. 'Hello Louis!' I said to myself. 'I must be in the right place.'

As I was admiring the beautiful room, a door opened and in walked a man. He was dressed in a much embroidered red jacket, well more like a skirt, as it went down past his knees as it puffed out from his waist. He had large puffy frills just above his hands, and his hair (or maybe a wig) was a brown curly mane that fell over his shoulders, halfway down his chest. He stopped and looked at me.

"You are welcome," he said formally as he made a slight bow of his head. "May I present myself. I am Pierre le Tessier du Montarsy. You are yet hours early for your appointment! The other members of the Council de Compagnons are not even here yet! By whose authority did you arrive here?"

"My name is Dewey, and I am not an apprentice of the Compagnons. I think I am here to speak with you alone, not the full council," I replied to him.

"How is this possible?" he asked, raising his voice slightly. "I have no appointments for the next few hours, and was planning to spend this time in my workshop working on something special for the king! I have no time for you!" With that, he began to turn back toward the door.

"Wait," I called out, "Perhaps if you see this it may change your mind." With that, I reached into my pocket, withdrew my Destiny coin and held it out toward him. He stopped, came toward me and took the coin. He looked at it carefully, and as he turned it over in his hand, I could see his face soften slightly into a small smile.

"Yes, well, this is unusual," he said returning the coin to me. "Come, follow me. We can talk in my workshop." With that, he turned and walked toward the door he had entered from. I followed him, and we ended up in a studio filled with all sorts of equipment and supplies for making jewelry. There was a kiln; a fireplace with a pot above it, I assumed for melting metals; a series of scales with weights; knives; tools; blocks of wood and wax; and containers filled with gold, silver and what looked like other ingots of metal. There was a small cabinet with a padlock that I assumed must hold the various precious gems he used. He motioned for me to sit at one of the chairs that were in the studio, a much simpler and more functional room than the one we were in before.

"This is most unusual," the master jeweler began. "I was coming down to work on something that the king has asked for. His third son from his mistress Madame de Montespan turns eighteen in a few months, and the king has asked me to prepare something worthy of the son of a king. His son's name is Louis Alexandre de Bourbon, Count of Toulouse. Although he was born a 'natural child', the king legitimized him at age three, when he was created the Count of Toulouse. At age five the king made him a grand admiral! Imagine, an admiral at age five! The power of a king! In any event, the boy has grown into quite a young man, and I believe he has a future as a military commander! So I am to create something worthy for such as him on this significant birthday. Is that why you were sent to me?"

"I don't know anything about Louis Alexandre or what would be suitable for him, quite honestly," I replied. "I think I am supposed to talk to you about what I feel would be a worthy 'masterpiece' as an apprentice of the Compagnons, something that has meaning and significance to me as I travel my own journey."

"But of course!" Pierre replied. "While it is normally the full council of master Compagnons that judge the apprentice's masterpiece, I am willing to listen. Perhaps you may have some ideas that will aid me in my task for the king. Please, begin." With that, he sat back on his chair, crossed his arms and waited for me to speak.

I got up from my chair, took a deep breath and began to speak. "My idea is for a man's signet ring. This ring and its image represent the authenticity and authority of he who would make his mark with it. Strong and powerful in meaning, yet simple and elegant in its lack of embellishment and precious gems. I propose a gold ring, yet not pure gold; one that has been strengthened with other metals so it does not bend easily. It is oval with a wide band at the sides narrowing at the base of the band."

I continued my presentation. "The face of the ring shows a common hummingbird, drinking from a flower whose stem encompasses the circumference edge of the ring. The hummingbird represents the will to do all you can to help others, and having it drinking from the flower shows it must take care of itself before it can care for others.

"The left side of the ring band has an infinity symbol, with an anchor embedded it in. This represents to always be strong, and as the anchor is heavy, to remember the weight of our responsibilities to our families.

"The right side of the ring band has a trident, symbolizing the discipline of self-rule and the three prongs of the trident representing health, energy, and fitness.

"Finally, engraved on the outside oval edge of the ring are the words worthy of a king's consideration; 'Even This Shall Pass Away'; reminding us that all things, good and bad, are temporary and will pass away. We are called to live our lives knowing this, and to respect each experience life gives us."

With my presentation complete, I sat down and waited for his comments. He sat there looking at me, not saying anything for what seemed a minute or so. He then got up, walked to the small locked cabinet and took a key from the inside of his jacket. He then unlocked the padlock and opened up the cabinet. Inside were many drawers. He opened one of the drawers near the bottom right corner and withdrew a gold ring.

"I made this ring some years ago," he started to say. "I felt inspired to make this, and the image is not one I would normally use or that for which the king would wish, but I felt that one day I would know the reason why." He handed me the ring. It was a gold oval men's ring with the image of a hummingbird drinking from a flower on it. There were no other markings on it.

"I think that I am to give this ring to you," he said. "I listened to all you said as you were describing what your 'masterpiece' would be. A master must have the ability to find appropriate symbols with meaning for the person who would wear what they would create. I believe you have this gift.

"Repeat those words worthy of a king again?" he asked.

"Even This Shall Pass Away."

"Of course, Even This Shall Pass Away. I can sense a powerful meaning in these words."

He straightened up, pulled his jacket smooth and looked at me. "The presentation of your masterpiece was inspired. Strong, simple and yet elegant. I agree that gold without the embellishment of gems is suitable for such a ring. The symbols are clear for all to see, yet it is their symbolism that resonates. A most noble masterpiece, worthy of a Master." He paused for a moment then continued. "I welcome you into the fellowship as a Master of the Compagnons du Tour de France! Therefore, as is the custom of the Compagnons, allow me the privilege to complete this ring for you so all will know you are a Master!"

With that, he removed his jacket, sat down at the workbench and fastened the ring into a small vise. With the ease and expertise of one who is a Grand Master Compagnon and jeweler to King Louis XIV, he picked up his tools and in a matter of minutes had carved both sides of the ring with the infinity and anchor symbol and the trident. He spent more time carefully engraving the words 'Even This Shall Pass Away' around the outside edge of the oval face. And inside the ring, he carved the symbol of the Compagnons; the letter 'C' inside a square, with lines radiating out to all sides from the center. Using a device powered by his feet, he began to polish the ring until it was smooth and gleamed in the light. He stood up from his bench, turning the ring over in his hand.

"I present you with this token in recognition of your rank as Master, and charge you to wear it as you continue along your Tour," he said formally as he handed me the ring. I put it on my finger, and it fit perfectly, as somehow I knew it would.

"Thank you very much," I replied with a deep bow. "I hope that your faith in me is justified. I will work to represent myself with honour and aid others along their own Tour."

"Becoming a Master is just a mile marker on your own Tour, signifying that you have achieved this level of success. The true legacy or role of a Master is to leave those to whom he is privileged to serve and teach better off as they travel along their own Tours," he said. With that, Pierre le Tessier du Montarsy, Grand Master of the Compagnons du Tour de France put on his jacket, bowed slightly and walked out of the workshop.

I was left alone in this workshop, looking at the ring on my hand. This had been an amazing visit!

# A Baptism Pool

I awoke in my bed. I looked over at the clock with groggy eyes. 4:52. Too early to get up, so I rolled over on my side and tried to get comfortable. The thumb on my right hand felt inward toward my middle finger. I felt something resist the movement of my thumb. I moved my thumb and felt the base of a ring. Immediately awake, I turned back to my bedside table, turned on the light, and as my eyes got accustomed to the sudden light I saw a gold ring on my finger!

I sat up and took a look at the ring. It was the ring from my dream! But if I had the ring, was it really a dream? There on the middle finger of my right hand was a gold ring with a hummingbird on the face. I saw the image of an infinity symbol, and yes, there was the anchor embedded in the base of the loop on the left side of the ring. I turned my hand slightly to expose the carved trident on the right side. And as I looked closely, I could see writing on the outside edge of the oval. I could not read what it said, so I got up, put on my reading glasses and looked closer. There engraved on the edge starting from the left side of the ring were the words 'Even This Shall Pass Away!'

"Too cool!" I said out loud to myself. The ring from my dream was there on my finger! I shook my head in disbelief, but it was there. The ring was real!

Sleep was out of the question now, not with this artifact from the time of Louis XIV on my hand! I sat up, took off the ring and carefully examined it. It was exactly as I had described it to Pierre, and now here it was in my hand. "What is the universe trying to tell you Dewey?" I wondered aloud, as I put the ring back on my finger. I got up, grabbed my journal and began to write.

> Well, crazy as it seems, here is the ring right in front of me. Exactly as I described it to the French jeweler! What was it that he said to me as he gave me the ring? Something about making sure that I leave people better off having served them? Was I now a Master? Is that what the ring signified? So weird! I will have to ask Mike how he can make all this happen. It really is a beautiful ring.

I paused, thinking of how mysterious this was. I closed my journal, looked at the clock. 5:17. "I am up now," I said out loud.

Later that week at the appointed regular time, I went to the park to talk to Mike. He was already sitting on our regular 'Bobby' bench as I approached. "How was your visit to the King's jeweler?" he inquired as I sat down. I held out my right hand with the ring on the middle finger in answer to his question.

"That is a beautiful ring," he said, holding my hand in his and examining the ring closely.

"I still can't believe I met some guy from the seventeenth century in a dream, but it must be real," I said. "It is almost too fantastic to believe!"

Mike just smiled back at me. "It seems that this ring with all the inherent symbolism it encompasses is just the thing for you," he replied. "Wear it well, and look to it often to remind you of the wisdom it contains."

"I will," I replied back to him. "It has a lot of positive symbolism in such a small space. Thank you for these special visits you have sent me on. I could have never imagined this ever happening! First the magic coin, then this ring..." I paused. "Thank you."

Mike smiled at me and nodded his head slightly, accepting my thanks.

We sat there on the bench for a few moments until I spoke again.

"I have been blessed with many good things in my life," I started. "I have a great wife and two beautiful girls who are fully into adulthood; I have had a very gratifying career, and I was able to sell my business and retire from full-time work, at age fifty. I have been told I have been given this 'massive gift', and now, meeting you at the time when I needed some help to find what was the next chapter in my life, well, it is just remarkable!"

Mike smiled and nodded his head again, accepting my words. I continued.

"I have not gone to church regularly in over ten years, yet I consider myself a spiritual man. Back when I was attending church regularly, I had been confirmed when I was fourteen years old but had never been baptized. I was baptized as a small infant, but never full body baptism. Not that I think you need to be. I believe that God knows the true you and your heart, whether or not you go through some ritual.

"However, back in early 2006, I was getting ready to be promoted to President of my company. Something told me in the back of my mind that before I accepted this new role, I should be fully baptized, you know, whole body, down in the pool. So, one Sunday afternoon in the spring of 2006, I had the full body baptism. I can't say it was some extraordinary, spiritual 'aha' event, but I am glad I did it. One of my friends at the time, Kevin, picked my baptism verse. I had not heard it before, but it was meaningful and spoke to my normally positive inclination. The verse was Philippians 4:8. 'Whatever things are true, whatever things are noble, whatever things are just, whatever things are pure, whatever things are lovely, whatever things are of good report, if there is any virtue and if there is anything praiseworthy – meditate on these things.'"

Mike looked at me thoughtfully. He said "Where we are today, what our destiny is, as the coin you carry so aptly says, is the result of all the choices we have made. Did your choice to be baptized result in all the other good things happening in your life? Who knows! What I do I know is that our destiny is the result of these choices, large and small, that we make continually. And the spirit in which we make these choices I think impacts this path to destiny. As for you, however, you are a young man. Your destiny has not been fully determined. You have chosen to consciously walk the path of the Sage's Journey."

I looked back at Mike, allowing his words to sink in. We sat there in silence for a few more minutes. Finally, I spoke. "So Mike, who do you have planned for my next visit?"

Mike began to speak. "As you travel on this journey, or any journey, you have to decide what you are going to bring with you and what you are going to leave behind. Consciously thinking about this, deciding what no longer serves you and what you want to bring into the future helps bring clarity to your thinking. With that clarity, you can better continue moving forward along your path. I am not talking about physical things to bring, like clothes or water. I am talking about the kinds of thoughts you think and the images you hold in your mind of yourself and of your future. An old proverb says 'As a man thinketh in his heart, so he is'. So for your next visit, rather than tell you much about the man you will meet, let me say this. He is not a very well-known person today, but his legacy was to help start a way of thinking that has impacted many millions of people. And you will meet him in a little town called Ilfracombe in the very south-west part of England."

"Off to England it is then!" I said. I rose from the bench, shook his hand and began to walk toward my car. 'England!' I said to myself, wondering whom it was I would meet next.

# A Drawing to Think About

This was the third time I was going to travel on some unknown adventure, so I was excited to get to sleep. As I lay in bed with the coin in my hand, I kept thinking about the simple proverb Mike had said. 'As a man thinketh in his heart, so he is.' I had read a lot of motivational books, and this sounded familiar. The Strangest Secret by Earl Nightingale talked about the six simple words, 'As you think, so you become' as a key to living. Napoleon Hill and his Law of Attraction said what you think about you can achieve. And the more recent book 'The Secret' said the key to success was to 'Ask, Believe and Receive.'

I smiled to myself. How many times had I said to my wife or my girls when we got the parking spot right out front of a busy shop or restaurant, or some very cool thing had happened to us, 'Law of Attraction girls! The universe is conspiring to bring us good things!' They would roll their eyes and laugh, but it happened to me all the time.

As I thought about this, I began to drift off to sleep. As I awoke, I found myself sitting on a rock on a hill overlooking a small harbor. A slight breeze was blowing on this overcast day as I wondered if this was where I was supposed to be. Eventually, I saw a man approach, walking along the pebbled path. He was slightly built, with a dark beard and a full head of bushy black hair.

"Why hello," he said. "I don't normally see anyone up here. Pleasant day, don't you think?"

"Yes, I suppose it is," I replied. "Good to meet you. My name is Dewey," I said extending my hand.

"James," he said. "James Allen, pleasure to meet you. Do you mind if I join you and sit down? I have been walking for near three-quarters of an hour and could use with a bit of a perch." I gestured to the spot beside me with my hand and James sat. "Thank you," he said.

"What brings you to this spot today?" James asked me.

"Well," I started, "you might find this a bit unusual, but I am on a bit of a journey. My friend calls it the Sage's Journey, and funny enough, I think I am supposed to be here to meet you!" With that, I reached into my pocket, took out my coin and handed it to him.

He raised his eyebrows as he took the coin from my hand and began to look at it. He turned it over, studied it closely and then smiling, returned it to me. "Destiny now is it?" he said. "Yes, well as your coin says, destiny is not a matter of chance, it is a matter of choice. Choosing what to think about, and what not to think about as well. I would agree with that. Now, what about this journey you talked about, this Sage's Journey. Tell me more about that."

I said that I felt this journey was one that would probably take my whole life, and that somehow part of what I was supposed to do was to be in some sort of service to others. What that service would be, I did not know. "But in my mind, I have these images of a lamp and a ladder as somehow being guiding principles as to how I should perform this service and travel along this journey." I said to him, trying not to sound like too much of a crazy person.

"A lamp and a ladder," he said thoughtfully, pausing for a few moments. "These are interesting symbols, yet more importantly they represent very powerful ideas. The words we say to ourselves and the thoughts we think about have the power to shape who we are and who we become. I wrote a small book just 2 years ago on that very subject. 'As a Man Thinketh' I called it. To be frank with you, I was not fully satisfied with the book. Oh don't get me wrong, I believe in the idea that we become what we think about wholeheartedly! Yet I think there was something incomplete about it. My wife Lily, however, persuaded me to publish it. And I am glad she did, as it sold well enough that I was able to quit my job as a private secretary, and now I can spend my time writing and working on a small magazine I started called 'The Light of Reason'.

"One of the things I have been thinking about is the power that images and symbols rather than just words have to shape our thoughts and what we eventually become. And what we choose NOT to think about is as important as what we choose TO think about."

"Well," I responded. "I believe I agree with you. Symbols and images have much power to convey ideas, quickly and at a glance." As I said that, I gazed down at the hummingbird image on my ring.

"If you would allow me to give you some advice," he said looking directly at me, "I think someone like you would benefit greatly from undertaking this exercise."

"Great!" I exclaimed. "I think that is, in fact, why we have met today."

"This exercise is simple, yet powerful. However, it will take you a few hours if you wish to get the full potential of its benefit," he said to me. "Are you willing to invest the time in doing this?"

"I am," I said firmly, nodding my head. "What do I do?"

"I want you to go home and get a sheet of paper. On it I want you to draw a line down the middle to make two columns. On the left side of the paper at the top of the column label it 'What I Shall Leave Behind'. On the top of the right column, label it 'What I Shall Take With Me." I want you to write all the things, ideas, attitudes, people or concepts that no longer serve you. Write down all these things that you do not want to bring with you on your journey in the left column. On the right side, write all the things and ideas that you feel will serve you, that give you energy and inspiration! These are the things you wish to bring with you moving forward. I would expect this right side list to be longer, but depending on what has happened to you in the past, the left side may have many items in it.

"Once you have written down these items, leave them for a few days. Allow your mind and the spirit of Infinite Intelligence to work on this list. After a few days, review your list once more with the idea to hone this list to only those items you truly wish to leave behind, and what you wish to bring with you.

"Then to fully bring the power of visual symbols into being, I want you to draw an item or symbol for each item on your list that represents what you wish to leave behind and bring forward. As you do this, you may discover that a single symbol can represent a few words. It doesn't matter what your artistic ability is, you will know what these items represent. Make sure you draw these items with as much colour and detail as you can. Your mind will take these images and do its work to somehow make these ideas come into being."

James continued. "Your drawing should be on a single piece of paper, and make sure to separate the symbols of what you wish to leave behind from what you wish to bring with you by a line, providing the barrier for that which no longer serves you to be kept from crossing into the area of that which will help you move forward on your journey.

"Once this drawing is complete, put it where you can review it each day. Look at the images and speak out loud what each represents. As you see the images and hear your words, this will do infinitely more to impress these thoughts upon your mind than simply just looking at the symbols will do. Do you understand?"

"I think I understand," I said. "It sounds relatively straightforward."

"It is not a hard task to do, but few take the time and put in the effort to do the simple things that can aid them most," he said. "Do this task; review your drawing every day and you will see how powerfully it can impact your life. You must choose to do the work. Remember, as your coin says, Destiny is a matter of choice."

James reached into his pocket and pulled out a small pocket watch. Opening it, he remarked, "Lily will be looking for me. I must be on my way. I wish you well on your journey. Remember, as a man thinketh, so he becomes."

With that, he stood up, nodded toward me and headed back along the path that had brought him to me. 'Well Dewey,' I said to myself. 'Looks like we have homework!'

I awoke the next morning and reflected on what James Allen had said. As I got up out of bed, I realized I did not know much about the man I had met in my dream last night. Normally Mike told me about who I was to meet, but all he had said was that I would meet him in England. Thinking back to where I had met James on a hill overlooking a small harbor, I realized that it could have very well been the coast of England. I opened up my laptop and looked up "James Allen".

'James Allen was an author who wrote many books, the most famous being 'As A Man Thinketh,' published in 1903. He was a pioneer of the self-help movement, and although he is not well known today, he inspired many of the more well-known self-help authors like Napoleon Hill, Dale Carnegie, and Earl Nightingale.' "I must read his book," I said to myself.

I closed my laptop and picked up my journal. I opened it up to a blank page and drew a line down the middle. On the left side at the top I wrote 'Leave Behind.' On the other side I wrote 'Bring with me.' I stopped and thought about what I would write. I knew the secrets to good brainstorming were lots of content, not making any judgments about what you write while you are writing, as one idea may lead to another, and to write non-stop for at least twenty minutes. The first five minutes were always easy, but the really good ideas came when you kept up the effort and kept writing. So I began to write.

After a while, I felt I was getting to the point of diminishing returns on my effort and looked at the clock. Only fifteen minutes! So I put my head down, reread my list, and sure enough, a few more ideas came out. Looking up again from the page I noticed that twenty-five minutes had passed in total. I closed my journal and went on with my day.

It was two days later when I opened up my journal and began to read the lists. I crossed out those that did not seem right, connected a few ideas that seemed to complement each other with a line and wrote a few more words that seemed to better reflect what I was thinking. This took about forty-five minutes. When I was done, I had a good list of what I wanted to leave behind and what I would bring forward. Now for the tough part, drawing these ideas into images.

"You went to business school, not art school!" I said out loud to myself. I could do a good stick person drawing, but I was not sure how well the other images would turn out. I got out a large 11" X 17" piece of paper and laid it sideways. I went and found some of the girls' old pencil crayons, sharpened them and began to draw.

The drawing went easier than I thought it would. I knew what the images were supposed to represent so they did not have to be perfect. I tried to use as much colour as possible as James had said. Time flew by, and almost 2 hours later I put the pencil crayons down and looked at the drawing. "Not too bad!" I said out loud. "Not bad."

As I looked at the drawing, I remembered the comment James had said about looking at each image and speaking out loud what the image represented to me. So I started on the left with what I wanted to leave behind.

An image of a desk, with a black chair and a gold nameplate that said 'President'. "Leaving behind my role as the President," I said.

A hand holding the rudder of a sailing ship. "Being in control."

A ball, a baby soother and a ringette stick. "No more responsibilities for small children."

A brick tower from a medieval castle, with a blue flag flying overhead. "The security of my role and identity at work."

A green face with the eyebrows scowling downwards. "Anger and envy."

A scale that read 220 lbs. "Being an overweight fat boy."

I stopped and reflected on these images. Not too many, I thought. Well, my life has not been too bad, so that seems right.

Between this group of items and the next, I had drawn a purple zigzag line, like a thunderbolt. Crossing this line was an hourglass, with more sand in the 'Bring with Me' section than in the 'Leave Behind' section. "Let's hope I do have lots of time ahead of me!" I said out loud. I began to look at the 'Bring with Me' images and began to describe them.

A sun shining in a blue sky. "Sunny days ahead!"

A brown leather bible. "Keeping true to my faith."

A globe. "The world is my oyster!"

A tan pith helmet with a brown band, like I had seen in all those jungle adventure movies. "A sense of adventure."

A gold ring with 'Even This' on the edge. "A sense of detachment and acceptance of what life will bring."

A glass of red wine. "Enjoy the pleasures of life."

A hummingbird with yellow and gold wings and a red head. "Do all I can."

A compass labeled N, S, W, E but with the word MORAL in the middle. "Be sure to mind my moral compass."

Black music notes on a staff. "Music."

An arm curled up with a large bicep. "Keep physically fit."

A black flashlight shining a yellow light, but tapering into a grey darkness at the end of the beam. "Have a plan, but don't worry about seeing the end."

A brown log cabin in a field of green pine trees. "Solitude and time alone."

A tan backpack with a Canadian Flag on it. "Travel light."

A face with a finger in front of its lips with the word bubble 'SHHH!' "Take time to be quiet."

A stack of scrapbooks. "Make memories."

A bunch of faces in a group. "Friends."

A stack of Canadian $100 bills. "Liquidity and plenty."

An infinity symbol with an anchor. "My girls."

A smiling woman's face. "My wife."

And finally, inside a red outlined rectangle, lightly coloured red inside with the words I AM in bright red. "My search for meaning."

As I sat reflecting on the drawing, I thought of all the various elements I had put on the paper. I had made sure that my list included all the areas of life that were important; personal, physical, spiritual, emotional, relationships, money and work. It seemed right, it seemed complete, and it seemed to represent what I really wanted. I smiled, and signed my name at the bottom. All art should be signed! I folded the paper in half and put it where I would see it and reflect on it every day.

# The Impact Circle

Once again, I found myself back in the park meeting with Mike at our appointed weekly time. I was excited to show him my drawing and to talk to him about my conversation with James Allen.

"How was England?" Mike asked as we sat down on 'Bobby's' bench. "Excellent!" I said. "I met James Allen, and he gave me not only some great things to think about, but he gave me homework! I spent hours this past week working on it. Here, I brought it with me," I said as I opened my bag to bring out the paper to show him.

Mike held up his hand. "It is not for me to critique your work. Remember, if you will, when we first started on this journey, I told you my role was to be your tour guide, and that we would not discuss in detail what you had learned from your various visits. 'It is not what you know, it is what you DO with what you know.'"

"No argument there. I've been applying and working from every experience. My journal is full of notes and ideas. I have been sure to write down my thoughts and things I have taken away from each person so I can look back and remember more fully what they have said."

"I knew you would," said Mike. "Keeping a journal of your thoughts and ideas is one of the best ways to learn and review what you have learned. An old saying goes that 'the palest ink is better than the clearest memory.' I am glad you are journaling your thoughts as you travel this journey.

"All whom you have met have given you things that will aid you along your own personal Sage's Journey. This journey will last your entire life, and the things you have received so far will be useful for many, many years.

"You have thought about how you are best suited to serve through the exploration of the Lamp, Ladder and Lifeboat paths. You have learned the importance of taking care of yourself as the best way to be of service long term to others, thus the idea of the trident. The ring you wear serves to quickly and simply give you counsel as to what you feel is important and provide inspiration at a glance. This drawing you have just done has helped bring into your consciousness those things you feel no longer serve you. This allows you to leave them behind, knowing they were important in the past, but no longer are part of your future. Thinking about what you want to bring forward, and speaking them every day will allow a greater chance that they will manifest themselves into your life.

"There is another tool that I would like to equip you with that will be helpful along your journey. I call it 'The Impact Circle'". He reached into his bag and pulled out a sheet of paper. "Allow me to explain it to you."

On the page he had taken from his bag was drawn a large circle with lines dividing it into three sections. However in the middle of the circle was a small circle labeled 'Image of Me.' The outside edges of the circle also had labels written above each of the sections. The section on the upper left side was labeled 'Vocation/Impact on the World.' The upper right section was labeled 'Key Relationships.' Finally, the lower section was labeled 'Just for Me – Personal Fuel.' On the side of the page beside the circle was the title 'Criteria,' and below that title were a few small sentences.

- Must be current with lasting impact
- Involves choice or change
- If you get it right, there can be a BIG impact on ME and others

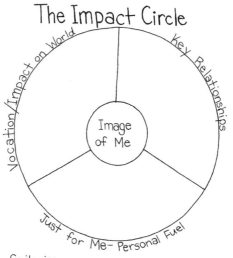

# The Impact Circle

Vocation/Impact on World

Key Relationships

Image of Me

Just for Me– Personal Fuel

Criteria:
- Must be current with lasting impact
- Involves choice or change
- If you get it right, there can be a BIG impact on Me and Others

Mike started to speak. "What I have given you is a blank template to help you complete this Impact Circle. Let me describe each of the elements in turn.

"The small circle in the middle of the larger circle labeled 'Image of Me' means just that. You are in the middle of the circle, joined and at the hub of each of the three sections.

'The upper left section is labeled 'Vocation/Impact on the World'. In this section, you list all the activities and things you can do to in your vocation or job and how you could impact the world. I use the phrase 'Impact the World' to highlight that these should be big and have a significant impact if you can get them accomplished.

"The upper right section labeled 'Key Relationships' is where you list all the most important relationships you have. Life is all about the relationships we have with others, so having strong, powerful and lasting relationships is key to feeling life was successful.

"Now notice how both of these two sections connect with you. To achieve success in these two quadrants takes energy, and this energy comes from you in terms of time, effort and activities. These sections draw energy OUT from you, and unless you replenish this energy, you will be unsuccessful in these two significant areas.

"That is why the lower section is labeled 'Just for Me – Personal Fuel'. It is also connected to you in the middle of the circle. It is here that you list all the things that you do just for you. These should be things and activities that bring energy IN to you, and I mean more than just food. What do you do to replenish the energy that you are spending on your Vocation and your Relationships?"

Mike looked up from the paper and spoke directly to me. "All of us direct our energy outward, into our jobs and the people we interact with. I have used the words 'Vocation/ Impact on the World' to highlight the significance of the activities you should do in this quadrant. If you are travelling at the high level of the Sage's Journey, you should have a higher order of impact that is more than just working for a paycheck. How can you turn your career into a calling that could impact the world? World-class activities take lots of energy. Similarly, having vibrant relationships takes lots of energy, more than just simply showing up. If you are going to plan on operating in these high energy using areas for the long term, you must have a plan to continually refresh yourself and keep your energy levels high? Do you understand?"

"I think I do," I said to Mike. "The idea of having a world-class impact has some appeal! What that exact impact is, I don't know, but I like the idea. And of course, having strong, deep relationships with key people I love is important to me. I never thought of those things as 'energy uses' or even 'energy drains', but of course they are! They take effort! I can see how this ties in with the trident idea that you need to take care of yourself if you are to take care of others. I like this Mike. It seems like a simple, yet powerful tool!"

"Take this paper with you," he said, folding it in half and handing it to me. "Use it as a template as you consider what should be in each of the three quadrants. This is a very personal exercise. There are no wrong choices to be made. However, consider carefully what you put into each of these sections. Be discerning, as a small number of high-quality impactful things are better than many items that disperse your energy. Take time to fully reflect on what you write."

"I accept the challenge Mike," I said. "I am looking forward to working on it and seeing what comes out!" I rose from the bench, shook Mike's hand, and putting the paper in my bag, began to walk away. 'This should be interesting!' I said to myself.

I set to work brainstorming and making notes in my journal on what I thought would fit into each of the sections. Having recently stepped back from a full-time career, I was having a hard time figuring out what to put in the Vocation/Impact on the World section. I was still involved with the company and wanted it to be successful, so I wrote a few things how I thought I could make an impact in my reduced role. The Key Relationships section was relatively easy. I knew who was important to me. But as I reflected on this list, if these people were so important, was I investing enough time with them? Most of these key relationships were family. What was visibly missing from this list were the names of a few close friends. I paused to consider why that was...

The 'Just for Me – Personal Fuel' section was interesting. I had spent lots of time in the past on self-development and self-reflection, so I knew what gave me energy. I also knew that improving fitness and losing weight had been a – 'to do this year, —For Sure!' item for the past decade. How could I be honest with myself and put that down without having a plan to make it happen?

Looking over these sections, a few themes were emerging. Also, the daily review of my drawing was starting to gel in a similar direction. If these themes represented what I wanted to bring with me, then if I was honest and consistent in my thinking, some of these elements should manifest into action.

I knew I wanted to have a small number of ideas that I could commit to doing. I also knew that each could be not just a word or two like 'eat less' and that a small phrase might work. "Power Phrases!" I said out loud. I liked that idea I thought as I sat nodding my head.

What actionable phrases would I write on my Impact Circle? I started to write.

In the Vocation/Impact on the world section, I wrote 'Share my passion; mentor/write.' 'Find a new job' was notably absent. I couldn't think of anything else for now, so I moved on to the next section.

In the Key Relationships area I had some insights. 'Allow space for my wife and I to be together.' That much was obvious. 'More time with my girls and Mom.' These were the key people in my life, and I realized I was not spending as much time as I wanted to do with them. Finally, as I did not have any names of friends that jumped out at me I wrote, 'Explore what I want in Friendships.'

I moved to the Just for Me/Personal Fuel section. 'Renovate my body to its healthiest state' was the first thing I wrote. I liked the word 'renovate'; it implied a multi-prong approach (the Trident was my inspiration here) to eating, exercising and taking care of myself. 'Begin the Sage's Journey' was the second item. The idea of this journey had given me lots of energy, and I was passionate to do this. 'Honour the backpacker in me', was the next phrase. I knew that I needed time on my own to reflect and write. I had done a few solo trips kayaking and camping and knew this solo time in nature gave me energy. Finally, I knew that I had to be a good steward of my financial resources, but how to write that down. An idea just came to me. 'Protect the Golden Goose.' I liked it! Making sure my finances were in order and safe meant the golden eggs that came from the goose would allow me the ability to take care of myself and others.

As I wrote these in each section, I decided to make a list of these items. As I did, I made slight modifications to the wording.

Travel the Sage's Journey (Lamp)
Allow time for my wife and I to be together
Ensure the safety of the golden goose
Create opportunities to be with the girls and mom
Explore what I want in friendships
Honour the backpacker in me
Renovate my body – health and fitness are key
Share my passion; mentor/write (Ladder)

As I looked at the list, liking what it said and meant to me, I had the sudden flash of realization that if I just moved a few of the phrases, it would create an acronym for the word TEACHERS! I rewrote the list in that order.

T – TRAVEL the Sages journey (lamp)
E – ENSURE the safety of the golden goose
A – ALLOW time for my wife and I to be together
C – CREATE opportunities for me to be with the girls and Mom
H – HONOUR the backpacker in me
E – EXPLORE what I want in friendships
R – RENOVATE my body – health and fitness are key
S – SHARE my passion- mentor/write (ladder)

I sat back, smiling and thinking that this just seemed right for me. This simple TEACHERS acronym would be easy to memorize. Reading it would remind me of the things that if I did would have a big impact on myself, and give me some direction and guidance of what things I should be doing. Just the idea to start the 'renovation' of my body was a big choice. How and with whom I would spend my time were also conscious choices I was making. And finally, could I see how this would have a big impact on me and others? Travelling the Sage's Journey I knew was sure to change me. Mentoring others was something I felt I could do. I had written a book seven years earlier that I called my 'best giver' rather than a 'best seller' and I had received many, many positive comments from people who appreciated one part of it or another. Was it time to write a second book?

TEACHERS: Travel, Ensure, Allow, Create, Honour, Explore, Renovate, Share. I began to read and say those words out loud over and over trying to memorize them and make them part of me. This way I could quickly remember my list and be inspired to work on them. "Travel, Ensure, Allow, Create, Honour, Explore, Renovate, Share...."

# The Monk's Scroll

It had been two very positive and fruitful weeks since Mike had given me the Impact Circle exercise to complete. I was excited to see him and tell him what I had accomplished.

"I see from the smile on your face that your homework was successful," Mike said, smiling himself as we shook hands and sat down on our bench. This spot had become quite comfortable over these past few weeks. Meeting here in the park on 'Bobby's' bench just felt right.

"It certainly was!" I exclaimed. "Working through the circle allowed me to get even more clarity as to what things I should be doing and I feel inspired! Do you want to see what I have written?"

"No," said Mike. "This was a personal exercise for you to complete. It is unique to you, and I do not want any reactions or comments I might make to come across as judgmental and make you second-guess what you have written. If you are pleased, so am I."

"Well, then I must at least tell you the acronym that came out of this exercise, as each word represents a unique phrase. The first letters of each word spell TEACHERS: Travel, Ensure, Allow, Create, Honour, Explore, Renovate, Share," I said somewhat proudly. "I have designed a small laminated card with all the phrases on it that I keep with me in my wallet. I even have a copy posted on the side of my computer!"

T - TRAVEL the Sages journey (lamp)
E - ENSURE the safety of the golden goose
A - ALLOW time for my wife and I to be together
C - CREATE opportunities for me to be with the girls and Mom
H - HONOUR the backpacker in me
E - EXPLORE what I want in friendships
R - RENOVATE my body - health and fitness are key
S - SHARE my passion - mentor / write (ladder)

"TEACHERS... interesting," Mike said. "The way your phrases create the word Teachers is itself not an accident I believe. I won't say more but I hope what you have written and learned will serve you well.

"I have been thinking of whom I should send you to visit with next. I think what this next person may have to offer you will be of great long-lasting value to you as you travel your journey. Your next visit will take you to a Monastery in France."

"France sounds great, but a monastery?" I said to Mike. "Sitting silently with a bunch of monks who don't say anything, and who spend their days praying and their nights chanting! I'm a spiritual person Mike; I have shared that, but I don't know if I am ready to be a monk!"

Mike laughed. "While there is something to be said for spending time in quiet contemplation, you are not going to be a monk; just to visit with one! It is the Prior with whom you will meet. His name is Guigo II, also known as Guigo the Angelic. He is Prior of the Grande Chartreuse, a Carthusian Order monastery of the Catholic faith located in the Chartreuse Mountains in South-Eastern France."

"Haven't heard of him, but I have heard of Chartreuse, the green French liqueur. I think I read that monks make this liqueur in their monastery. Maybe these monks might be alright guys after all," I joked.

"I am sorry to disappoint you," Mike said laughing. "While the monks of Chartreuse do in fact make the liqueur, they did not start doing that until the mid-1700's. Guigo II was a 12th-century monk, so you are 500 years too early!

"Guigo II was the author of a small book called 'The Ladder of Four Rungs', written in about 1150, known more recently as 'The Ladder of Monks'. It describes a ladder or series of stages that monks should progress through in their contemplation of God. I thought that since your own path has an element of a ladder in it, that Guigo II would be an interesting person to visit. You are not, however, going to meet him to learn about contemplation and prayer. I think what he may have to offer you may be more suited to where you are at this stage along your journey."

"OK, no drinking with the monks, I understand, but is there anything else I should know?"

"For now this is enough. Enjoy your visit… Brother Dewey!" With that, Mike got up. I got up as well, shook his hand, and we walked our separate ways. 'Well Guigo,' I said to myself. 'I am looking forward to what you have to say.'

That night, I fell asleep with the coin in my hand and awoke sitting on a stone bench outside a walled building. A large iron gate was placed in the wall, ornate yet simple in its design. The gate was closed, and I sat on the bench not far from it.

Above the gate was a stone arch, carved with a large cross. Above it in a semi-circle were seven stars, three on each side and one star just above the vertical spar of the cross. The bottom of the cross was enclosed in a circle. Below this were the Latin words: - STAT CRUX DUM VOLVITUR ORBIS -

I sat admiring this unique artwork when a man in a homespun wool robe with a cowl hood came walking up the path behind me toward the gate. He stopped in front of me, giving me a better observation of him. His pale garment was contrasted by his very dark black hair, cut short as if a bowl had been used on his head as a guide to the barber.

"Bless you and greetings friend," the man said. "Why is it that you sit in front of the gate? What do you seek?"

"It is not what but whom I seek," I replied to the monk. "I am looking for Guigo. Would that be you?"

The monk laughed cheerily. "No, I am not Prior Guigo. He is the leader of our order, and not usually given to foraging for mushrooms in the forest," he said, indicating his basket. "My name is Brother Gervase. Is the Prior expecting you?"

"I am not sure, I don't know," I said. Brother Gervase did not move, he just stood looking at me. A few moments passed and I had an idea. "Here," I said, reaching into my pocket and pulling out my Destiny coin. "Please give this to him. Tell him that I wish to speak with him. Dewey is my name." With that, I handed Brother Gervase the coin.

Brother Gervase took the modern coin, examining it, then looked at me, wide-eyed with astonishment. "I will take this and give it to Prior Guigo," he said to me, moving toward the gate, which swiftly opened at his knock. He glanced at me as he moved inside.

Not much later, I looked up to the sound of metal scraping to see Brother Gervase's tonsured head poking out from the doorway. "Please follow me. The Prior will see you," he said, gesturing for me to follow him. I rose and walked through the gate into a tidy courtyard surrounded by a covered promenade. I followed him down the cloister and into a hallway.

We walked down the plain, stone-walled hallway toward the end of the corridor. There was little ornamentation or decoration on the walls as we walked down the hall. We came to a wooden door, having a knocker with the same cross in a circle I had seen outside. This time the cross was made of metal. It was the only art or decoration I had seen in the place. Brother Gervase picked up the bottom of the circle and knocked on the door softly.

"Enter," said a voice from behind the door. Brother Gervase opened the door and motioned for me to enter, closing the door behind me, leaving me alone with a man sitting at a wooden table.

"Welcome to the Grande Chartreuse Monastery," the man said rising from his chair and giving me a slight nod of acknowledgement. "I am Prior Guigo, actually Guigo the second, but you may call me Guy. Have a seat if you will." He motioned to a wooden chair in front of his desk.

Prior Guy also took his seat. He was wearing the same homespun robe with a cowl hood as Brother Gervase had been wearing. Prior Guy wore a green sash around his waist as a belt, and around his neck was a black iron cross with the circle below it, hanging from a worn leather strap. Prior Guy seemed considerably older than Brother Gervase, having thin, silver hair and a weathered face. I noticed a distinctive front gap in his remaining teeth, as he smiled, looking at me.

"I was intrigued when Brother Gervase handed me your coin," said the monk. "I do not recognize it, nor could I read the inscriptions as they are in a language I do not know. However, it was the eight-pointed cross and the stars that circled them that caught my attention and made me impatient to meet you."

"Perhaps when you were waiting outside the gate you saw our Cross, the symbol of the Carthusian Order of which the Grand Chartreuse belongs. Did you see it carved above the gate? It also has a cross with a ring of stars." Prior Guy paused, waiting for me to reply.

"Yes Prior Guy, I did see it, along with the inscription in a language I could not read," I replied. "What does that inscription say?"

"'Stat crux dum volvitur orbis.' It is the motto of our order, and it means 'the Cross is steady while the world turns.' It is our role as a Holy Order to be a constant, steady influence in the world, even as the world changes. The Cross surrounded by stars calls us to look heavenward, while the base of the cross in the circle represents our dwelling here on Earth. Tell me, what does the inscription on the back of this coin say," he asked, handing me back my coin.

I picked up the coin and read the inscription to him. "It says, 'Destiny is not a matter of chance, it is a matter of choice; it is not a thing to be waited for, it is a thing to be achieved.'"

Prior Guy closed his eyes and remained silent for a moment. He opened his eyes, looked at me and spoke. "These are wise words; truly. Our eventual destiny is a choice that all must make, and he is wise who takes action to gain that destiny here on earth. Thank you for sharing those words with me.

"As monks, our spiritual destiny is to follow the ladder ever higher as we try and come closer to God. The story of Jacob's ladder as told in Genesis describes how God had allowed Jacob to ascend into heaven. We as monks must also strive to climb this ladder. We must begin on the first rung, Reading, where we spend time learning and reading God's word. We then must climb the second rung of Meditation; thinking and reflecting on the words we have learned, searching for their meaning. As we ascend to the third rung, Prayer, we are called to spend our days in constant prayer, asking for guidance and the wisdom of insight. Most are only able to climb up to this third rung. It is the fourth and final rung, that of Contemplation, that many try but do not succeed in achieving. We must become awakened to the non-dual experience of oneness with God. A monk's yearning must become so strong that as he feels he is no longer able to climb any higher, God in his heaven and in his wisdom reaches down to him. You cannot climb up this fourth rung, God must reach down to you and pull you up." Prior Guy closed his eyes and remained silent.

He opened his eyes and looked again at me. "Forgive an old monk for giving you such a sermon! Perhaps you will now enlighten me," he said. "Why is it that you have come here today?"

"I'm not so sure myself," I said to the old monk. "I am on my own journey and have been working on better understanding what it is that I am to do. It has something to do with a ladder and a lamp."

The old monk smiled warmly at me. "All of us are on a journey of some sort," Prior Guy began. "Some seek to take that journey here in a monastery, devoting their lives to the Sacraments and prayer. Others take their journey travelling to foreign lands looking for adventure. Most do not even realize that whatever they do, or wherever they are, they too are on a journey. What you seek is the same as what all searchers seek... Wisdom."

"What do you mean by wisdom?" I asked, intrigued by his comments.

"Wisdom is difficult to define as a single thing. It is more than having knowledge and good judgement. It is more than just experience and intuition. It is more than just right words and actions. It is in the earnest seeking of wisdom itself where it is most often discovered.

"I was wondering why you came to see me today, and now I think I know why," Prior Guigo continued. "Recently, one of the monks found an old, small vellum scroll. It was found wrapped in cloth inside one of the ancient walls that was being torn down so we could make renovations to the sanctuary. This scroll was hidden between the stones, and when it was discovered, it was brought to me. Who knows how long it had lain there, undisturbed? It contained words in a language I did not understand. The heading on the top of the scroll, however was in Latin. It reads 'Sapientiam Quaerere,' which means 'Seek Wisdom.' Now that I have seen your coin, the writing on the scroll looks very much like that!" Prior Guigo pushed back his chair and went to a wooden chest in the corner. He opened up the chest and removed a small scroll, less than a foot long.

The calfskin vellum of the scroll was smooth; it had not hardened or cracked with age. The cream coloured vellum surrounded a pair of black ebony wooden dowels. I noticed that the ends of the wooden dowels of this scroll were quite different. One end of the wooden dowel was a simple round ball, while the other end of the dowel was carved with the intricate face of a cherub. The top dowel had the cherub on the right side and the ball on the left, while the bottom dowel had these ends reversed. Thus when the scroll was closed, the cherub and the ball both were together on each side, facing one another. The scroll was held closed by a green and gold braided leather cord.

Prior Guigo handed me the scroll. I untied the leather cord and carefully unrolled the scroll. Unrolled it was about 10" in length. I saw the Latin heading, Sapientam Quaerere, written in ornate script. The shocking thing was that the words below were written in English!

"Can you read these words," inquired the Monk.

"Yes I can," I replied. "This is amazing!"

"Please read them to me," Guigo asked. I began to speak.

"Chronicles 1:11-23

Since this is your heart's desire, you have not asked for wealth, possessions or honour, nor for the death of your enemies, and since you have not asked for a long life but for wisdom and knowledge... therefore wisdom and knowledge will be given you. And I will also give you wealth, possessions and honour...

Proverbs 4: 6-7

Do not forsake wisdom, and she will protect you; love her, and she will watch over you. Wisdom is supreme; therefore get wisdom. Though it cost all you have, get understanding.

James 3:17

But the wisdom that comes from heaven is first of all pure, then peace loving, considerate, submissive, full of mercy and good fruit, impartial and sincere

Proverbs 2:6

For the Lord gives wisdom; from his mouth come knowledge and understanding

Proverbs 16:16

How much better to get wisdom than gold, to get insight rather than silver!

Proverbs 19:8

The one who gets wisdom loves life; the one who cherishes understanding will soon prosper."

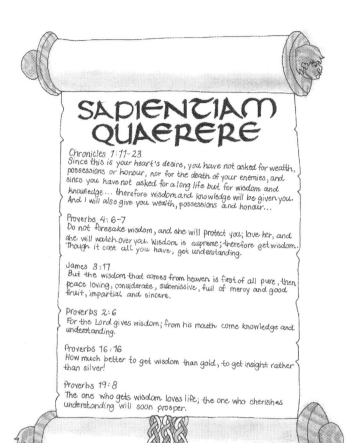

# SAPIENTIAM QUAERERE

**Chronicles 1:11-23**
Since this is your heart's desire, you have not asked for wealth, possessions or honour, nor for the death of your enemies, and since you have not asked for a long life but for wisdom and knowledge... therefore wisdom and knowledge will be given you. And I will also give you wealth, possessions and honour...

**Proverbs 4:6-7**
Do not foresake wisdom, and she will protect you; love her, and she will watch over you. Wisdom is supreme; therefore get wisdom. Though it cost all you have, get understanding.

**James 3:17**
But the wisdom that comes from heaven is first of all pure, then peace loving, considerate, submissive, full of mercy and good fruit, impartial and sincere.

**Proverbs 2:6**
For the Lord gives wisdom; from his mouth come knowledge and understanding.

**Proverbs 16:16**
How much better to get wisdom than gold, to get insight rather than silver!

**Proverbs 19:8**
The one who gets wisdom loves life; the one who cherishes understanding will soon prosper.

As I finished reading, I noticed that Prior Guigo had again closed his eyes. I could see his lips moving slightly as if speaking to himself. After a minute or so he opened his eyes. A small tear fell from his right eye.

"I have been blessed today by you," said the Monk. "These words I have read before in the Holy Scripture, but having them together on this scroll, in a language that only you could read is a special gift." He lifted his eyes toward heaven and raised his hands slightly. "I thank you Lord for these your words, given to me, your humble servant."

He looked back at me and said, "I believe this scroll was meant for you. I am pleased that I could be here to share this blessing. I wish you to take it and meditate on these words every day, for they will help you find the wisdom that you seek." With that, he carefully took the scroll from my hands and rolled it up. He took the green and gold braided cord, gently wrapped it around the scroll, tied the ends and handed the scroll to me.

"May these words help you to find the wisdom you seek. Do not keep this scroll to yourself, but share these words with others so that they too may find their own wisdom."

He got up and led me to the door. "I must meditate on these words I have heard today. Bless you, my son, as you travel along your journey's path."

He opened the door and nodded his head slightly toward me. I returned the gesture and walked through the doorway, down the dim corridor, and into the light of the cloister.

I woke in my own bed. I looked at the clock. It said 3:16 AM. Was this real or was it a dream, I asked myself. I noticed then, in the red light of the alarm clock, lying on my bedside table was a round white scroll wrapped with a cord.

# Some New Ink

I carefully untied the leather braided cord and opened up the scroll. The vellum was still soft and supple, and the ink writing was distinct. Surprisingly, there were no tears or signs of aging that I could see on it. I read the text a few times during the early hours of the morning. I laid the scroll down on the table where I was sitting, picked up my journal and opened it up to the next blank page. I began to write.

> I just met Guigo II, a monk from the 12th-century. He gave me this scroll titled 'Seek Wisdom.' The title was written in Latin, but the words of the text written on it were English! Weird!

Guigo said that what I was searching for on my journey was what everyone was looking for; Wisdom. The scroll is a collection of bible verses all describing wisdom in various ways. Wisdom was better than gold! Wisdom is Supreme! Love wisdom and she will watch over you! But none of them say what wisdom really is.

He told me that I should read the scroll every day, so I will make sure I put it near my drawing so that I can look at both of these things each morning.

Sometimes I had to pause to consider how many unique learning experiences I have had since meeting Mike. I wonder how they will help me as I walk this Sage's Journey. Am I really cut out to be a Sage? What else must I learn along this path? But I am committed to this. To reassure myself, I whispered softly: 'Have the discipline of the Trident Dewey! Stick with the program!'

So for the next days before my meeting with Mike, I continued to look at my picture every day and talk out loud what all of the elements meant. I read the scroll out loud every day as well. I found my mind did not wander as much when I was speaking out loud. I also had bought a small journal where I began to record my weight every day, and to record if I had gone to the gym or not. I needed this piece of forced discipline to help keep me on track. I put my drawing and another small laminated copy of my TEACHERS card in this weight journal so I could review them every day as I recorded my progress on my physical renovation.

Finally, it was my day to meet Mike. I was anxious to speak with him so I was already sitting on our 'Bobby' bench when he arrived. "Hello Dewey," he said to me as he sat down. "Did you enjoy the monastery?"

"I did! I was given a scroll, and although I have been reading it every day, it still seems like it is written in riddles," I said to Mike. "It calls me to seek wisdom, but so far I'm not sure I have found any!"

"I would disagree with you," said Mike. "I think you have gained more wisdom than you think. Aristotle said knowing yourself is the beginning of wisdom. During this time we have spent together, along with all your experiences and learnings from your past, you have gotten to know yourself much more than you think! You have spent time considering what path you will travel, and have come up with the Lamp and Ladder idea, and rejected the Lifeboat.

"You have rediscovered the need to have the discipline to take care of your body and your health so you will have the energy to travel the path. You wish to serve others, thus the symbol of the hummingbird on your ring has special meaning to you. You have visualized all you wish to leave behind, and have drawn clear images of what you want to bring with you. The TEACHERS acronym you developed has given you some clear directions of actions you should take.

"I think that the 'riddles' that the scroll describes to you are not riddles at all. They ask you to continue in your search for wisdom, and that the pursuit of wisdom is a prize more valuable than any worldly possessions. Wisdom is not a prize you collect or something that you can own. Wisdom is like a winding yet never-ending path. You look ahead and glimpse what looks like the prize, but when you arrive, you find that while you have gained much, there is still more valuable treasure ahead in the path you have yet to travel. This is one of the blessings of the journey!"

I reflected on what Mike had said. It was true. I did feel a more confident sense of where I was going these past few weeks. Maybe I had already unwittingly learned some of the wisdom of the Sages!

"People of all time have valued wisdom," said Mike. "In fact, I know of a learned professor of history who would say that wisdom is one of the Four Universal Values that have been appreciated by people throughout history. Professor Rufus Fears passed away in 2012, but he left behind his thesis that the Universal Values of All People of All Times were; Wisdom, Justice, Courage, and Moderation. That itself is wisdom worth considering."

Wisdom, Justice, Courage, and Moderation. Interesting ideas I thought.

"We are now coming to the end of our time together Dewey," Mike said to me. "I think you have come to a point where you need to travel your journey alone, learning and reflecting on where you have been so far, and moving forward with confidence along your path. Your 'lamp of wisdom' will not show you all of the path, but with this lamp, trimmed and full of fuel, you can see far enough ahead of you to walk in the light on the rest of your journey."

"There is however, one more person I want you to visit. I have made an appointment for you in the Trinity Bellwood section of Toronto for this time next week. You are to meet a very special woman. Her name is Alanna, and she is a tattoo artist."

"A tattoo artist!" I exclaimed. "Mike, I am fifty-one years old and have made it this far without a tattoo. I have never thought of getting a tattoo, and if I were honest I would admit that I am afraid to get one! And now you expect me to go and get a tattoo?"

"You have been travelling this journey, and I think you are committed to staying on the path. Am I right?" asked Mike?

"Yes, you are right about that," I said to Mike. "I am committed to following through on this Sage's Journey. But a tattoo? That is just… so… permanent!"

"I have arranged for you to meet Alanna for a few reasons," said Mike. "First, she is an amazing world class artist, a woman excelling in a field that is dominated by men. She is making a name for herself through her ability and creativity; she is a woman worth spending time with.

"Secondly, you have spent these past few weeks learning and exploring many new ideas, and have discovered the power of representing an idea with an image or symbol. The Lamp, the Ladder, the trident, the hummingbird, the infinity symbol; not to mention all the images you have drawn that you wish to bring forward with you, are all powerful symbols. The Carthusian cross, the navigational compass on your Destiny coin, the phrase Even This Shall Pass Away; all these symbols invoke passion and give you meaning when you look at them. They give you energy! Finally," he said with a grin, "I have already paid for your appointment!"

"Mike, you are pretty convincing," I said. "But a tattoo... I am not sure about that."

"The permanence of getting a tattoo causes you to consider if you are committed to walking the Sage's Journey," Mike continued. "It may seem like an unusual idea, but as I have come to know you, I think this permanent visual reminder, more than a scroll, a drawing or even a ring, will serve to help you stay committed to the path you are on.

"You have learned much and have grown a great deal in our time together. You are free to make your own decisions and to do as you please. It is my belief that this final act of commitment; knowing you and your personality as I think I do; will become a proud visual reminder of the path you have committed to journey on. I will not pressure you to do something against your wishes. This is your journey, not mine. Never allow anyone to make you act in a way that is not of your choosing. You have a week to decide if you wish to go ahead or cancel your appointment. I am proud of you Dewey and all you have accomplished. You have great things ahead in your future."

Mike stood up, reached into his pocket and gave me a slip of paper with the details of the tattoo shop and my scheduled time. "It has been a pleasure to have been your tour guide on your journey Dewey. We will not meet again. Know however, that I will be observing you in silence as you strive to achieve great things. I wish you well on your journey!" Mike leaned over and embraced me warmly. Afterwards, he shook my hand for the last time and walked away.

For the next few days I considered Mike's comments. A tattoo! I had never, ever, considered a tattoo before. As I allowed his comments to linger in my mind, I began to warm up to the idea. There was nothing wrong with a tattoo. A little ink was normal nowadays. It was not just sailors and bikers who had tattoos! I began to think more about it. Why not?

Now that the idea of a tattoo was confirmed in my mind, I had to consider what tattoo I would get. I thought of all the various symbols and their meanings that I had developed over these past few months. Was there a single symbol? Could I make a few symbols combine into a meaningful piece of art? Yes, I wanted it to be art. It had to have meaning, but it also had to be beautiful.

The night before my appointment, I still did not know what the image would be. I had wrestled with the idea for days, and I was still not clear. So that night I decided when I went to bed to fall asleep with the Destiny coin in my hand. Every time I had fallen asleep with it, good things had happened. It took me a while to fall asleep, but eventually I did.

I awoke with a start early the next morning. It was still dark, but I had seen an image in my dreams that I felt perfectly represented all I wanted in the tattoo. I turned on the light, went to my desk and took out a sheet of paper. I began to draw the image that was in my mind. When it was done, I looked at it. 'Well Dewey,' I said to myself. 'I hope that the artist can take this and make it beautiful.'

I went down that afternoon to Bellwood Tattoo. As I went in, I felt a sense of calmness and certainty fall over me. I walked up to the counter. "I have an appointment with Alanna," I said.

"I'm Alanna. It's a pleasure to meet you," this slim, red-haired woman said to me. "So what are we doing today?"

I showed her my sketch and described what I wanted. I told her the meaning and significance of the image and what it meant to me. "I like those ideas," she said to me. "A tattoo should represent something special and personal. I think I can work with this."

We went over to her table. "Where would you like the tattoo to go?" she asked.

"My right inside forearm," I said. "That way I can see it anytime I want. I am fine with it being visible to others, but I am doing this for me."

She took an alcohol swab and cleaned my arm. Next, she took a disposable razor and shaved the area of my right forearm. "I think I am going to do this freehand, single needle," she said. "I know what you are looking for and I have a good idea of how to give you a beautiful tattoo."

"You are the best, I'm told. Do your best!" I said.

She nodded appreciatively, dipped her needle into the ink and began to work. "This should not hurt too much," she said as she leaned into her work.

I watched as she began to move the needle slowly across my forearm. 'I am really doing this!' I said to myself. As the small lines began to form into an image, I smiled. I was truly committed to travelling the Sage's Journey.

# *Epilogue*

A month or so had passed since getting my tattoo. It had healed nicely and I often found myself looking at my arm, this constant reminder of the journey I was on.

I was now in the habit of every morning describing my picture of what I wanted to bring with me on this journey and of reading the Wisdom quotes from the scroll out loud. I had made copies of these Wisdom quotes, and had given them out to those whom I thought might appreciate them.

I had not seen Mike since our last meeting in the park, so it came as a surprise when I open up my mail and found a red envelope with my name and address on it. There was no return address. The stamp interestingly enough was the image of Mr. Spock from Star Trek.

Inside the envelope was a plain note card that contained this hand-written message.

Hello Dewey;

I understand that you did get your tattoo after all; well done! I know you will have chosen something meaningful.

Here is a quote from an unknown author that I wanted to share with you.

"Today I will meet the world as it is,
Greet others where they are,
And be all that I am."

Lastly, allow my final words to you to be the same the final words spoken by the Buddha: "Just Do Your Best."

Your 'tour guide' and friend;

Mike

# Notes on the Text

This little fable was born from a desire to share some of the insights gained during my journey so far. I hope that in reading it, you have found some parts worthy of reflection, or even of inspiration. Although it is a personal document, about myself, it is an open invitation to being mindful about your own journey.

All the characters in this story do or did exist. I have tried to create believable and realistic dialogue with respect to each individual's distinctive voice and message. Any errors or omissions are unintended.

## Mike and Dewey

I have had the pleasure to work with a great coach, Mike Boydell, since back in 2009. He initially worked with my partner and I, as we were about to buy the business we were working in from a pair of brothers. My partner and I had different styles that could well have been conflicting over time. Working with Mike allowed us to better understand each other, and make the best of our different management styles. It worked outstandingly well for over seven years, until we eventually sold the business to the next generation of leadership.

I worked with Mike as my executive coach throughout 2012 and again in 2016/2017 as he helped me work through my transition to 'what's next' as I prepared to step down from actively running the company. From Mike I received the Impact Circle exercise, and it was also his idea to draw the Leave Behind/Bring Forward diagram.

So, it is not too much of a stretch to figure out that I would have the 'tour guide' in the fable named Mike.

The name Dewey also was coined by Mike. In one of our sessions, (my journal has it April 2017), Mike said that he had noticed that I kept lots of lists, and had tracked my progress over the years. "It seems Dewey, your cataloger, is in charge a lot," he said, challenging me that day. That is how the name 'Dewey' came about. Plus, I had never read a fable with the main character named Dewey, so I thought this would make him unique!

Finally, the quote at the end of the book from 'Mike' written on the note card by the "unknown author" is actually a quote from Mike Boydell.

## The Sage's Journey

I first read about this idea of the Sage's Journey in December 2009 in a book called "Fathered by God – Learning What Your Dad Could Never Teach You," by John Eldredge. He described the various life stages, with the final stage being the Sage's Journey. I had often thought about what this book meant to me over the past years. It became the basis of how I identified with my own journey, and in turn became the central motif of the book.

## Axiom Destiny Coin

This is a real coin! I backed the developer of this coin, J. Alan Garber on Kickstarter in 2016 and carry this coin with me. The description of the coin and the meaning of all the elements are directly from him. I just made up the part about it being magic!

## Rumi, the Lamp and the Ladder

I had never heard of Rumi until I was reading over the Christmas holidays in 2016 a book called "The One Life We're Given" by Mark Nepo. I often record notes from books I read into my journal (see, Dewey does appear a lot). It was toward the end of the book (page 278) where I read for the first time the quote by Rumi, "Be a Lamp, a Lifeboat or a Ladder." As I recorded my thoughts each day during the holidays (I do my annual goal setting and reflecting over the holidays), I kept talking about and developing the Lamp/Ladder idea. As in the fable, I realized that the Lamp/Ladder idea gave me energy and so I started to use it.

## Rob Roy, Navy SEAL

Rob is a real person. The description and details of him from the fable are all true, including the fact that his face is on the covers of the PS2 SOCOM and SOCOM II video game jackets! I met Rob when I went on a Navy Seals experience in September of 2008. It made sense in the fable for Mike to have gone to this event, but in actual fact it was me. I was terrified of what these SEALs were going to do to us, and they warned us... hard... that we better show up in shape! I had 9 months to get from what was an over 200 lb. fat-boy into fighting SEAL shape. I started eating better, worked out hard, ran in combat boots, did a couple of sprint triathalons and came to Coronado, California in the best shape of my life. The lowest weight I got down to (as recorded in my daily weight journal, yes Dewey shows up a lot!) was 158.2 lbs.

As 2018 rolled around, I once again found myself over 220 lbs. (how did that happen?!). I had weight loss as an annual goal for the past ten years with no real results, but reflecting that this was the ten-year anniversary of my Navy Seal adventure gave me the kick in the ass to get back on the program. I came up with and actually put a symbol of a trident in my weight journal. I labeled the prongs Health, Energy and Fitness (as in the fable). I had however labeled the shaft of the trident as Vibrancy. As I was writing the fable, I changed it to what I think is a better label, Discipline. I am using the image of the trident to focus my physical transformation efforts.

Rob's comments about the three keys a Navy SEAL knows being a solid and clear Mind: a fit and capable Body; and a strong and positive Attitude I took from the descriptions in his company's website. His company is also real, called SOT-G (www.sot-g.com) and these descriptions were taken from their "Tip of the Spear" 360-degree physical training program.

## Pierre le Tessier du Montarsy and Louis Alexandre de Bourbon

When I was looking for a character to develop the ring, I discovered Pierre, jeweler to King Louis XIV. King Louis did have an illegitimate son, (he had lots actually), named Louis Alexandre de Bourbon who he made Count of Toulouse at age three. All the specifics of these men are historically accurate. Pierre was a member of the very real Compagnons du Tour de France, which is still in existence today. I found it quite a pleasant coincidence that this jeweler was a Compagnon du Tour de France, and Dewey was on a journey (or a tour…). The Count of Toulouse did go on to become a real Admiral of the French Fleet, (not just being named an Admiral at age five). Louis Alexandre, Count of Toulouse was commander of the French fleet at the largest naval battle during the War of the Spanish Succession. His flagship, the Foudroyant, (Thunderbolt in English), led at the Battle of Malaga on August 24, 1704.

I thought it worked well to have Pierre, the jeweler, to get ideas for a birthday present for someone who would eventually command the French Fleet. The ideas of the infinity symbol and anchor and trident seemed to work nicely.

The gold ring is quite real. I had it custom made in 2016, and I wear it on my right hand every day. It has the hummingbird, is ringed with the words "Even this Shall Pass Away", but the only difference is that the infinity symbol with the anchor is actually on both sides of the ring;, there is no trident on the right side. And inside the ring it is engraved 'Pettes', not the symbol of the Compagnons.

## James Allen

James Allen was one of the pioneers of the self-help movement. His book "As a Man Thinketh" was published in 1903. He really was not very satisfied with it. It was his wife Lily's persistence that got him to publish it, and it continues to sell today, over 100 years after his death. I took some poetic license to create the visualization drawing as something he probably would have suggested.

Many years ago, my dad gave me a blank journal for Christmas 1982 when I was sixteen years old. Inside it were these very inspiring words from a father to his son.

> "All that a man achieves and all that he fails to achieve is the direct result of his own thoughts. In a justly ordered universe, individual responsibility must be absolute.

A man's weakness and strength, purity and impurity are his own, and not another mans. They can only be altered by himself, never by another. His condition also is his own. His suffering and his happiness are evolved from within. As he thinks, so he is; as he continues to think, so he remains.

In the spirit of Christmas 1982. Love always, Father."

It was only years later when I read "As a Man Thinketh" and found this exact quote in it that I realized that my father had copied it and had passed it off as his own words. Oh well, they are good words regardless of where they came from! It's a remarkable coincidence that we both found our way to that book by Allen, and were inspired by it.

## Guigo II The Angelic

I first read about Guigo II, called the Angelic, in a book called "Christian Meditation – Experiencing the Presence of God" by James Finley. I read this book in 2009, and it is was there that I found out about Guigo and his work, 'The Ladder of Monks.' I had made notes in my journal about this author and his idea of the four rungs of Reading, Meditation, Prayer, and Contemplation. As I considered who would be a good person to give a list of bible verses on wisdom, Guigo came to mind. Who better than a monk (with the coincidental ladder tie-in to the story) to give Dewey the bible verses!

The monk that Dewey meets at the gate who introduces him to Guigo, Brother Gervase, was also a real person. The original version of The Ladder of Monks was a letter written by Guigo II to Brother Gervase titled "Letter of Dom Guigo the Carthusian to Brother Gervase, about the Contemplative Life." It was written about 1150, and it was years later that Guigo's work became known as 'The Ladder of 4 Rungs' and now more commonly 'The Ladder of Monks.' Guigo describes Brother Gervase as the one who "...stole me, O happy theft, from the slavery of Egypt and the delights of the wilderness to make me a soldier in the ordered army of God." I took literary license in making Brother Gervase subordinate to Guigo. Only after his death was Guigo called "the Angelic."

As I researched the Carthusian order, I discovered the symbol of the order, the Cross with the Stars surrounding it and the base of the Cross in the middle of the circle. This seemed to tie in well to the stars on the coin as reason for Guigo to give Dewey an audience.

As for the list of Wisdom quotes, I put the list together myself in March 2017, and every morning I do read this list, out loud, in my office as part of my morning reading and devotions. It is on a simple piece of paper, folded in 4 to fit into a book. I don't have a fancy calfskin vellum scroll, with a pair of cool, (I think they would be cool!), carved ebony wood dowels. I liked the image of the angelic cherub facing a simple ball, on opposite corners yet when rolled up they were together on both sides. In my mind it represented heaven and earth facing each other... Plus a special scroll should have more than a couple pieces of wood on each end.

# Alanna the Tattoo Artist

As I approached the end of the fable, I had Dewey meet a woman, whose art and insightfulness provided a fitting finale to the parade of characters that he encountered. She was the one who synthesized the symbolism of his journey, and transformed it from the abstract into the real. I came up with the idea to end with Dewey getting an undisclosed tattoo so that it could be left open to interpret and wonder what the image might have been. This felt like the right kind of closure.

I found the name of Alanna Mule from Bellwood Tattoo in Toronto from an article that had appeared in the Huffington Post on 10/06/2015, written by Priscilla Frank. The article was titled "25 Badass Lady Tattoo Artists from Around the World." Alanna was listed as #21.

I have never met Alanna, but chose her for a few simple reasons. First, if she was good enough to get in an article with the top 25 Badass Lady Tattoo Artists in the World, she was good enough to ink Dewey's tattoo! Second she was in Toronto, so it made getting Dewey there easy.

## The "Bobby" Bench

I liked the idea of having Mike and Dewey meet in a park. Nature seemed to provide the right setting for these conversations. There is a real 'Bobby' bench. It sits in Montebello Park in St. Catharines, Ontario facing the band shell. The plaque on the bench reads "Donated to the City of St. Catharines in Loving Memory of VILMA STEPHANIE HEFLER (BOBBY) 1921 – 2003 Who Loved

This Park." Vilma Stephanie Hefler was my Auntie Bobby. Auntie Bobby is one of my all-time most favourite people in the world. She was important and significant to me; giving love and affirmation and letting me know I was prized by her. I was her 'little tiger.' She is one of the angels that continues to watch over me on my journey, so it felt right to have her there watching as Mike and Dewey spoke.

## Closing Thoughts

I hope that as you have read this book I have not come across as someone with all the answers, I don't have all the answers! As Robin Sharma, the Canadian author and motivational teacher says, "I'm no Guru!"

One of my TEACHERS items is "Share my passion – mentor/write." This book is the output of trying to be faithful to what has been my personal journey thus far, and to share with honesty and transparency some of the things that have worked for me in hope that some ideas will spark with the reader.

It was a fun experience to have written this book. Thank goodness for the journals and notes I have been making for years. They helped the ideas for the book flow smoothly and quickly. And finally, thank goodness for Google! It is remarkable, to sit in a log cabin in the woods and find all these interesting historical figures and learn about them, making them a part of my journey! I have not been to a library in years!

Printed in the United States
By Bookmasters